Stay Ahead of the Game

Reading between the Lines and Filling In the Blanks

VOLUME 3

Arlindo Fernandes

iUniverse®

STAY AHEAD OF THE GAME
READING BETWEEN THE LINES AND FILLING IN THE BLANKS

iUniverse books may be ordered through booksellers or by contacting:

iUniverse
1663 Liberty Drive
Bloomington, IN 47403
www.iuniverse.com
844-349-9409

ISBN: 978-1-6632-0943-6 (sc)
ISBN: 978-1-6632-0944-3 (e)

Library of Congress Control Number: 2021915062

Print information available on the last page.

iUniverse rev. date: 08/23/2021

Contents

Introduction

FROM THE MOMENT WE WON the sperm marathon, the process of our becoming something extraordinarily amazing began. And sooner than we thought, nine months had passed and there we were at the peak of another milestone holding a permit to join the crowd of heroes at birth for the continuity of the unique and special journey—the human quest. Surrounded by astonishing amounts of love, nurture, care, and devotion, we're to dance with amazement at the mysteries of life. As we gather the ingredients that will make us even greater winners and empower us to deliver our packages, we grow, learn, and evolve.

During childhood, we were restrained by our parents' rules, which made us long for freedom. Surprisingly, as we began experiencing life our way, we realized that life came with joy, love, peace, and brotherhood as well as surprises, which we despised passionately. Some surprises tempered our confidence and power of deliverance. And when we got our freedom, we realized that its definition had terms we weren't aware of or had interpreted wrongly. The unwinding of events we couldn't control and the laws of life became more brutal than our parents' harsh rules, and we were confused. Life was beautiful, comforting, appealing, and rogue, but on the other hand, it had elements that were impossible to understand. We wanted to embrace fun, but our responsibilities, stresses, and frustrations increased, and that made fun go home. Our responsibilities drained our time and energy; it felt as if life had betrayed us unmercifully.

It all happens to be so because for reasons we've yet to understand—and we probably never will—life's full of mysteries. Some seem to work against us and make us want to give up on our quest for excellence. Fortunately, our determination and perseverance gave us courage to play, dominate, and stay ahead of the game; we didn't want to hear about hard, impossible, or invincible. We're always focused on bringing out the best in us to please our moms and dads and prove that we were not mistakes and that we're seriously committed to unleashing our potential and see how far we can fly. We learn from every game we play. We're always eager to discover what's behind the horizon, and we're ready to embrace the journey to a new dimension. This attitude and our determination and eagerness to dominate in the game turn us into veterans of life. Now, experience makes everything easier and we rely on wisdom to allow our intellects and grit to guide our destiny. We now use our superior skills to reach greater heights and collect the trophies.

Yes, we've come a long way and packed all kinds of tools and experience to be distinguished heroes who pave the way for the next generations and teach them better, easier, and more-gratifying ways of life.

Sadly, life throws us curveballs in the worst ways. The tools and the experiences we've accumulated are still our best supports, but we need supplemental empowerment to dodge the balls when we should, catch them when we must, and not be bruised when we get hit by them. But that supplemental empowerment is not easily seen and even harder to grab. And yet our confidence in gaining a victory is not shaken. When we learn to read between the lines and fill in the blanks, we acquire that supplemental empowerment. Responsibility comes with that empowerment.

1

The Game Evolves

The first three years of life are full of joy, love, care, gratitude, and happiness, but then life begins to deal us cards we don't like, and we find ourselves unablc to keep up with life, let alone get ahead. Since everything is in motion, we'll inevitably face headwinds, be exposed to tailwinds, and be knocked down often. We're prone to sweets and potions of life by its natural dynamic and the consequences of our attempts to make something new, better, and different. We give the last drop of our blood to stay ahead of the game, but we face failures at times and feel disempowered.

But as winners, we can' t let anything keep us from winning trophies. Sure, our workload increases as the game evolves, but so do the means for our success despite the mysteriousness of our journey and the turns we have to make. Lucky for us, our game came this way. The constant change of reality is a gift, not a curse; it keeps our minds, bodies, and spirits going stronger as we find ways to move along and stay ahead though we might not notice this.

This product of our evolution has made our lives easier, more interesting, and more fun than those of our ancestors. The further back we look, the greater the astonishment, and the further ahead we look, the greater the amazement. We should be glad for changes in the game. However, we can struggle with change because we can resist change; we're comfortable and familiar with where we are. This biological phenomenon evolved with us and will never become extinct. When we go to new places, no matter how confident we are about getting there, we can still feel anxious about the trip. The more we ask people for directions, the more we display our state of anxiety, concern, and frustration.

And as we head home, our emotional state doesn't change much. Sure, we made it there, but on the way back, we travel cautiously and look for the familiar; only then do we start relaxing despite the help we get from GPS. Resistance to change is part of who we are.

We do not know with certainty what changes will occur, and we fear the potential consequences of our actions even if we are in charge of the changes that come our way. When there's no option but to accept change, sooner or later, we adapt to that new reality and change becomes normal.

Let's take all of life's changes and mysteries as sources of inspiration and embrace the game with a determination to become excellent not when all goes well but all the time. We have the abilities to analyze what lies in front of us, predict its outcome, and change it to our desire.

Reading between the lines and filling in the blanks make us invincible beasts facing life with confidence and certainty. Besides, change is a good thing, so we should not fear the changes and evolution we go through. If we remain confident that we'll thrive, we will.

2

Who Could You Be?

We are products of our environment, which itself is a product of many factors such as the economy, government, society, and preceding generations. To be born and raised in a good economy is to have the possibility to turn natural skills into excellence. To live in a democratic country with the freedom to pursue happiness is to have the tools to turn any zero into a hero. But when we live in a corrupted country ruled by tyrants, the laws can limit our freedom, quarantine our wishes and desires, and turn us into submissive, apologetic individuals with internal rage. We're not who we should be. Oppression alone could easily make us troublesome individuals. And if we grew up in a ghetto and were molded by stress, frustration, and depression, we become belligerent and short tempered and cause trouble.

And then, the big giant—media enhanced by technology—has the biggest influence on us regardless of our surroundings. And to make matters worse, media has the gaming industry as their right-hand buddy. Their combined forces are an impossible monster in our living rooms. Even if this monster has not rerouted our personalities, it has made us very dependent on TV and video games—beautiful devils—and it leaves us with no time to develop our skills.

As powerful and as deep rooted as they've become, the media and the gaming industry will always have enough water to grow. Only if they couldn't meddle with us regardless of our age, race, or background!

We don't need to be geniuses to recognize the poor ability of youngsters to hold a straight, face-to-face conversation or engage with confidence in any activity that requires good verbal skills. Their online altercations spray madness and hatred and spit venom. They're not getting their teeth broken or their noses bloodied, but they become idiots feeding their personalities with rage, which leaves scars rather than loving memories.

It seems that as a result, each generation is cursed in worse ways than previous generations had been cursed. The world is pouring dangerous agents into our personalities in many ways; what we eat and drink and what we watch, hear, and do release invisible arrows of failure and disempowerment like guided missiles. We need to upgrade our defenses to stay the course and become successful.

We can't control all the factors that contribute to our personality development, but since the stakes are high and the bars have been raised, it's becoming mandatory to know who we are and who we could be and get to work becoming our best selves while keeping our heads above water.

Gene editing came too late for us. I'm not sure we should feel sorry about that, but let's unwrap the gifts of our ancestors. If we like them, we should see what we can make out of them. If we don't, we have to find ways to bring delight to them. In either case, we should bring out the best in us. It doesn't matter who we are or became; when we hit our fifties, it's too late for reframing our personalities; we've joined the club of too-old dogs that can't learn new tricks. Therefore, you youngsters must consider your natural skills and compare yourselves to your achievements to get a clear picture of who you could be. And then with determination and grit, you can lean on history and experience to take yourselves to the elite level before it's too late.

Finding out who we could be implies fighting with tooth and nail, determination and perseverance to achieve the greatest success our genes and surroundings allow. Wherever we are, we're surrounded by fallen stars whose bad personalities whisked the red carpet from under their feet. Day and night, sick minds terrorize the world and stop great, young minds from flourishing all the way to moms killing their own innocent angels. On the other hand, there are ordinary cursed souls on forgotten streets of lost cities who rose from the ashes to become millionaires and role models as well as others with an abundance of bad genes who turned themselves into beacons of excellence.

We can always improve our personalities; we're human beings, the ultimate species. We carry infinite treasures in our souls that we can release for our benefit. Our greatness is not to be kept dormant; it must be set free for cooking the best dish to feed all including ourselves.

Once you embark on the journey to excellence, you'll be touched by glory and excitement. Embolden yourself to read your ancestry and analyze your surroundings to find a strength to eliminate the demons on your path. Be an inspiration, a beacon, a star. Reach into your unlimited powers to bring the best out of you and become the best you.

3

The Power of Knowledge

ONE THING WE PICK UP by instinct and dance with throughout life is knowledge. We recall its importance when we're standing next to somebody who knows just about nothing or when we've been victims of ignorance. It's not by chance that children ask too many questions and get in trouble for touching everything; they simply cannot help it. They thirst for knowledge, a wonderful tool that enables them to experiment with confidence, and experience is itself knowledge. Without these two, we wouldn't be independent creatures traveling beyond the horizon and achieving impossible dreams.

During our initial learning phases, we're at the mercy of our ancestors, economic power, time, and our environment. If most of them are good, we're on the road to great experiences. Then comes the second phase—the acquisition of knowledge.

Acquired knowledge is a gift we give ourselves after we've taken control of our destiny. It's the checkmate, the magic trick of all games. It wears tiny, sophisticated scopes with telescopic lenses. It's the greatest instrument yet in helping us read between the lines and fill in the blanks especially in gray villages, where the real action takes place. It's such a shame we're becoming more and more dependent on the easy-does-it philosophy while the laws of life demand that we throw ourselves into the wild to have a vast knowledge through experience for our empowerment and excellence. If we could only learn with the masters of the gray area—governments and politicians! But since we'll survive one way or another, why bother with knowledge and experience? As someone once said, "What's Google for?" Well, here's why you should bother with knowledge and experience:

If you refuse to broaden your knowledge, you're shooting yourself in the foot before the marathon starts. You're crazy, lazy, or both. To be ahead of the game is to know that your enemy (life) will strike first. Acquired knowledge is your weapon. To experience a lot is to be confident and ready for the battle. If this is not convincing enough, ask a forty-seven-year-old who knows jack about cooking how it feels when his wife's not cooking. He might ask you to not even come over. Leave the couch and celebrate life! (I wish my son Chris and his online buddies and many addicted gamers around the world would listen to this. Me too though not as badly.)

The More We Know, The More We Realize How Much We Don't Know

Knowledge is infinite, but that shouldn't trouble us. What should trouble us is all that we don't know because that can kill us. The more we don't know, the more we need to know. Today, we need to be able to understand the digital world. We must upgrade ourselves every day just to catch up. And as we manage that we become happy. We think we know a lot until a thirteen-year-old shows us how much we don't know about our smartphones and other such devices. We can be happy catching up with technology and the craziness of world until we find out the technology giants are combining forces with the military for total control of the world and society, that the government has underground cities and bunkers for its members' safety in case of a nuclear attack, and that only the richest and best of the best minds will be selected to colonize Mars.

Every day, we celebrate new discoveries, but that makes us realize how much we don't know. Technological advances are about to face a setback because the language of science—mathematics—isn't evolving fast enough to allow us to understand the algorithms of our new discoveries and their application to our lives. We suffer the consequences of ignorance—ours and others'.

It was a beautiful night—clear skies, a pleasant temperature, a nice breeze. The new day had just started to move into the second hour of its twenty-four-hour journey. I was driving, and I turned the radio on and found a song that matched my pleasant mood. I was cruising on backroads, happy as a bird; I felt that life was good. I might've exceeded the speed limit here and there but never by much or for long, but blue flashing lights appeared in my rearview mirror and were catching up to me. I pulled over, stopped my car, and made my arms visible to the officer who was approaching me.

"Good morning, Mr. Fernandes."

"Good morning, officer," I said though I hated it when people "Mistered" or "Sirred" me.

"I had to stop you because you were going seventy-five miles an hour."

"Seventy-five? Really?"

"Can I have your license please?"

"Yes," I answered. I got my license out of my wallet and handed it to him.

A few long minutes later, he returned and gave me my license and a ticket. "I wrote you a ticket for speeding and texting."

"I wasn't texting. I was making a phone call."

"It's the same thing—using a communication device while operating a vehicle."

"I see everybody everywhere talking on the phone while driving."

"It's a violation. You can fill out the back and send it to court for a hearing or pay it in twenty days. Have a nice day."

Two months later, I was in court. I was sure I'd get that ticket wiped off my record, which had been clean for almost seven years, and I had talked with a lawyer about the ticket. I explained my reasons to magistrate for disputing the charges and mentioned the officer's explanation of using cellphones while driving.

I was basically saying to her that the officer who had stopped me was a lunatic, but she shed some light on my ignorance: "It's not illegal until you're charged with other violations," she explained. I felt stupid and wanted to punch myself in my head.

My ignorance had cost me $105. My clean driving record was stained, and my auto insurance went up for six years. I vowed I wouldn't collect any more traffic tickets.

Ignorance affects people everywhere and every day. Here are some examples.

Whether or not Donald Trump was the legit winner of the US's 2016 presidential election, Russia was meddling in that election through Facebook to drive people to Trump instead of Clinton. And so did fake news. If voters knew that, they might've voted differently even though the outcome of meddling might never have been known.

- Our poor knowledge of our partners is the number one reason for the high rate of divorce.
- The more we don't know about our enemies, the harder it is to strike their weakness.
- The more we don't know about the beast, the higher the probability of our being hurt by it.

What we don't know can destroy us and others. Before we pay a high price for voting foolishly, we should realize that life is a beast of many heads and hidden horns.

Knowledge is a savior, while ignorance is a killer. Honor your gifts by continually learning for your empowerment, advancement, and excellence.

Filtering Knowledge

In this era of information overflow, filtering content is crucial. Otherwise, we'll believe idiots and even smart idiots who invented their own stories or cut and pasted news from accredited journalists, bloggers, and news stations and then brushed them with lies and fantasies for their own benefit.

When the credibility of stories seems based on the numbers of likes, comments, and shares instead of on their merits, it could be fake news. The authors (or criminals) get cash while we make costly mistakes and die of thirst because our knowledge doesn't hold water.

The news stations are all about "Be the first … Correct later." And you shouldn't blame them; there is competition in all sectors of life. Whoever sticks his or her head out first gets the attention and the prizes.

Don't internalize stories you've just read or watched even when they come live from the source. Give stories time to marinate before you cook them. Read between the lines, and fill in the blanks with a brush of a broad spectrum of knowledge. Expand your knowledge, and become able to spot fake news, things that sound too good to be true, and hidden messages or treasures behind real information.

Knowledge Sharing

The attacks of 9/11 could've supposedly been stopped if there had been better knowledge sharing. Since then, we've been sharing more even among enemy countries. As a result, many terror attacks didn't happen. We continue to discover plots and catch terrorists before they make deadly moves.

Scientists and research groups have been sharing their discoveries openly and sooner. From the powerful media to ordinary individuals, we're sharing events as they develop. We've embraced the sharing of knowledge like madmen. Alleluia! The big brains finally realized that the sooner we know, the better, and that the more we know, the more empowered we will be to make the best decisions.

Share what you know with the world, and most important, apply it to your daily activities.

Knowledge Application

Knowledge will illuminate our paths, enlighten our brains, and make us first stringers rather than backups sitting on benches. The world's changing fast and continuously, and we must tag along. The danger is that we're victims of a double-edged sword: too much of good and bad things. It's sliced and diced us severely. Now we must be vigilant and walk away from realities that can slice and dice us again.

Your knowledge should inspire you to become a shining star, not a beast in the abyss or a desperate loser. The older you are, the higher the expectations are of you. Age means wisdom, and wisdom means a greater power and success. Constantly use your knowledge to stay on higher ground for all that's great; you'll inspire others more and shine brighter.

When you apply wisdom and confidence to your knowledge, you'll win big as you're less likely to…

Be mad at the world. When you apply wisdom and confidence to your knowledge, you'll understand that everyone has a viewpoint, a personal agenda, and a different way of achieving goals. Some of the ways could be obstacles in your path you'll have to overcome.

Curse friendship and employment. When you apply wisdom and confidence to your knowledge, you'll understand that friends can betray friends, employers must make a profit off their employees, and that employees aren't actually any company's best assets.

Let your relationships, finances, and retirement plans be in disarray. When you apply wisdom and confidence to your knowledge, you'll empower yourself to live in the gray area more than in the black-and-white area and to use others' experiences to your advantage.

Hate governments, despise politicians, and curse the rich. When you apply wisdom and confidence to your knowledge, your critical thinking and the right application of your knowledge will remind you that governments abide double-standard laws, politicians have families to feed, and wealthy peoples' job is to make money at all costs. You'd also understand no matter how much you wish it were the other way around that there's just one planet to share with black and white, rich and poor, the smart and the idiotic, babies, children, teenagers, adults, the elderly, and terrorists and peacekeepers.

Another benefit of knowledge application coupled with wisdom and confidence is that you will live on your own terms rather than on others', especially important when their philosophies are rooted in bias, prejudice, hatred, and misconceptions.

In 1983, my friend qualified for a three-year scholarship in Cuba. At that time, he was living with his girlfriend and didn't want to send her back to her mom for the three years; he wasn't comfortable leaving her without security and a shoulder to lean on. He had many friends and family he could've asked to look after her, but he chose me. As it wouldn't be an extra burden for me, I gladly accepted his request. I was after all as good as a family member, if not better. We'd been hanging out after work every day at his house playing cards, watching TV, and so on. We didn't have any secrets—definitely not dark ones—and we were truly like brothers. His girlfriend was friendly and always welcomed me as her boyfriend's best friend and treated me always as her brother-in-law.

Since we lived just a few houses apart, she'd be knocking on my door as needed. And she did that many times after her boyfriend left. Some days, she'd chat with me and then drag me to her house for more chatting. Sometimes, I stayed to keep her company late into the night. She always made it comfortable for me to stay, and I always made it comfortable for her to come over. We were better than lovers! Apparently, that was an innocent mistake. Or was it a mistake?

Unbeknown to us, neighbors spread rumors about our behavior, and I still don't know if those rumors reached her boyfriend's ear. Years later, I found out that my friend's brother got into an argument with him and called him stupid for letting me be her caretaker and insinuated I'd been sleeping with her while he was gone. After learning that, I reexamined our behavior and concluded that the neighbors had concluded that there must have been fire after seeing the smoke she and I were creating, but she and I had never been on fire.

My friend had been wise to have trusted in me. He probably took into consideration what others might say, but he was confident in the arrangement. His girlfriend had felt safe, protected, and respected under my wings, and I was proud to have honored my promises. The three of us didn't let our neighbors' biases and prejudices dictate our behavior.

Apply your knowledge wisely and be the captain of your ship. Knowledge is the only true measure of your success. The more you know, the stronger your tools are for building your castle. You'll live longer and happier lives than your ancestors did because you know more than they did, and you'll apply your knowledge for your advancement better than they did.

Luckily for us, right when we think we know enough, the curiosity bug whispers in our ear, "You need to know more." Fortunately, we obey. We know about black holes and the big bang theory. We've gone to the moon, and we're preparing to go to Mars and then migrate and colonize it; we study outer space to learn more about it.

If you know nothing, you'll become a slave to robots instead of being their master. Your smartphones and devices are running your life already, aren't they? Only knowledge can save you and make you the king of all jungles.

We have to be able to read between the lines and fill in the blanks with the assistance of the philosophy of life in gray areas and respect reality. The philosophy in gray areas forces us to see what's beyond and to take necessary measures for success. Those we admire—our idols and stars—use this philosophy as their guide and inspiration. We can be special, idols, shining stars too.

We shouldn't conform our lives to the black and white. No matter how great it is, we can make it better. Life's like a tree of knowledge all can climb. In black and white, we're taught to collect low-hanging fruit, easy and safe to pick. In the gray area, we're told to climb the tree to collect fruit higher up, which is hard to pick but sweeter and more nutritious. Only knowledge can teach us the secrets and reason life in black and white does not want us to climb the tree.

Get on with a program of excellence, and honor yourself. Learn with animals, rumors, gossip, good and bad friends, media, the internet, and science. Each has a valuable lesson that will empower your reading between the lines and filling in the blanks. Place knowledge above everything else, and worship it with passion and devotion. You'll not regret it.

4

Teenagers' Curse

AFTER GOING THROUGH BIOLOGICAL BURNING flames of hell, it sounds like a joke to say the torture goes on for teenagers, but it's not. This tragedy is real, almost impossible to believe, and hard to digest as different whips come through the gates of life and society and swing unmercifully. Since the teen ages are part of the journey for all, we can only hope that families help their teens sail through rough waters and that society understands their internal chaos, pain, and sacrifice.

Sadly though, teens haven't been getting the help and understanding they need. The opposite is what they've been getting without a sign of relief. Fighting biological changes is a continuous struggle, and battling social dynamics and human hypocrisy is a challenge quite impossible for teens to endure.

If you're a teen, take it from me… What lies ahead is greater than you can imagine. Unfortunately, it comes at a sharp price; be careful or you could be severely cut, and healing your wounds could be quite impossible for you to endure. Read on and search as much as you can for ways to empower yourself for your independence and excellence or you'll forever be victims of the teenagers' curse. Here are some powerful curses.

Government

Governments do what they can to turn teenagers into good citizens including passing laws to keep them in line. Lucky are those who have family support and can maintain a straight path to success, but in general, teenagers are whipped by laws that they consider stupid and unfair. Then there are games going on behind the scene, where the young and powerful are trapped for political and economic gain.

Teenager who were sentenced to time behind bars based on the needs of young minds and strong bodies are whipped by curses, and the chain of this game extends beyond big dogs. Cops are on the lookout for the right teens to feed the need. Teens' recklessness and bad behavior are a recipe for an unfair roller-coaster that has its first stop at the jail. Their immaturity doesn't come to rescue them; it rather pushes them into the path of the train of chaos.

Therefore, regardless of how hard it might be for you to steer your behavior away from troublesome roads, you have to try your best to follow the rules. Empower yourself to see trouble and troublemakers from miles away, and then run as fast as you can from them.

Media and Marketers

The media influence is the obnoxious, crazy uncle whose family tries to keep their children away from. Unfortunately, parents and teenagers lose. The media is too powerful. Backed up by science and technology, they dump their hypnotizing and contagious philosophy on teenagers to turn teenagers into their best friends. They invest tons of cash on research to keep teenagers glued to the content they offer; the larger the audience, the greater the ratings and the money from advertisements.

Marketers have strategies for turning teenagers into potential buyers. They know teenagers are easily seduced with cool stuff and without thinking twice buy any ideology offered. They're easy targets. As the world's becoming increasingly dominated by market economy (capitalism), teenagers find themselves pulled in all directions by media and marketers.

Teenagers' and Parents' Relationships

I don't believe relationships between teenagers and parents will ever get better. Both sides have their lives driven by an infinity of intruders. Chaos, stress, frustration, and loss of control are pretty much dictating everyone's life. Teenagers are under stress right when they need compassion and understanding, and they can seek that online. As unfortunate as this is, it's the norm in every family. This normalcy will get only worse because there are too many players in the game of life. The tragedy is that parents are trapped and can't find a way out despite their expertise in life let alone teenagers' lack of experience and the ability to make reasonable decisions.

The teenagers' complaints that parents aren't there for them is real and universal, yet they're not free to go. They're indeed guilty as charged. If you warn teenagers that they have nowhere to run, no place to hide, they say, "I don't care." If you explain to them that their bad behavior brings consequences, they say, "Who cares?" Teens have no idea that they're their own worst enemies fighting in the jungle and blindfolded by the curses of life. And most of us parents—to our shame—don't know that either.

What's worse is that on the one hand, some parents don't know better, and on the other hand, teenagers are bombarded with all kinds of biological changes and stabs from their own demons making it impossible for them to be humble, reasonable, respectful, and good listeners—the necessary elements for a good relationship. As a result, too many factors build rip currents on the parent-teenager relationship ocean. Wouldn't it be nice to reverse the curse?

Reversing Curses

How can teenagers reverse curses if they don't know they're cursed? They can't, but they must to become successful adults. Therefore, teenagers must accept their harsh reality and then start reversing curses. Some curses are biological and thus almost irreversible, but teens can fight them off and get some relief.

Teens, I'm not sure how big of a winner you can be as you find yourselves fighting on many fronts; the outcome of a fight is known only after it's over. This gives confidence to your determination to fight curses and reverse them. Let's say you carry belligerent genes. The chances are you're going to engage in lots of fights and probably make a few trips to an emergency room to fix a broken nose, spend days in the principal's office, or even get expelled from school due to disorderly conduct, fights, and arguments. In this case, avoiding actions that lead to trouble and choosing levelheaded friends will serve you better. Fighting the agents driving you to such bad behavior is worth it. Your belligerent actions could still affect you but not ruin your life. And with some luck and determination, this could be a significant step in keeping your belligerent personality dormant or watered down.

Nothing says that you can't fight biology and turn yourself into a peaceful and harmonious person. Other biological curses such as a poor intelligence quotient, poorly developed eyes and ears, and bipolar disorder and schizophrenia require a delicate fight. Alone, you won't reverse them, but it's worth seeking help for them. Find ways to go over, under, or around your biological shortcomings; give it all you got.

Being in a wheelchair doesn't mean staying at home paralyzed. If you allow every situation to take a piece of you, by the time you're twenty-one, your life will be out of control, and by age twenty-nine, there'll be nothing left of you. So engage in any and all empowering activities. Teenagers' curses can drive you nuts and disempower you. Your duty is to fight them all, reverse the ones you can, and seek help for the ones you can't.

We've realized that you teenagers are capable of performing extraordinary duties that require discipline, coordination, dedication, skill, and decision making in the military and other venues. That means you have what it takes to avoid the nets and whips of curses whether biological or humanly created. You just need to take matters into your own hands and learn to spot threats to your opportunities. Empower yourself to fight the ideology of people dictating how you must live, and then seek help from people who care about you.

Don't fool yourself or let anyone fool you into thinking that you can be a teen expert in reading between the lines and filling in the blanks; you can't. Yet you don't need to wait until you're a fully grown adult to start taking charge of your destiny and developing the necessary skills for reading between the lines and filling in the blanks. The way media and marketers are after you, you might never be an adult in charge of your destiny let alone able to develop the necessary skills for reading between the lines and filling in the blanks. For that, it becomes mandatory to emancipate yourself from distraction and technological slavery and to always remember that there is no curse you can't reverse or a spell you can't suppress.

And if you find yourself unable to take charge of your destiny, worry not. Ride the waves safely. When you get ashore—to adulthood—pack all your experiences into a large backpack and restart your journey strong. Soon after, you won't remember any curses of your teen years.

5

Government

MANY THINGS ARE PHENOMENA OF a symbiotic relationship that allows for mutual survival and success. In such a reality, harmony should rule, but for the most part, it never does. Governments and people fit into this reality. Whether governments grew too big and too powerful or people became too demanding and ignorant, both are constantly bad-mouthing and throwing rocks at each other. Each has to attend to the demands of the other and work together on making dreams come true. This last part is what creates problems in this relationship because the actions of one can impeded another's advancement.

With tons of factors that contribute to the degradation of such relationships, we the people need to chill out and focus on making our dreams come true taking into consideration that yes, governments became too powerful and people became too demanding and ignorant for reasons neither could control completely.

The new times have been dropping responsibilities onto the shoulders of governments some by people, others by foes and friendly nations, and some by the constant change in the dynamics of life and governing. Every nation has been dealing with economic turmoil, social unrest, crime, poverty, immigration, competition, wars or consequences of wars among so many other phenomena that make it just about impossible for governments to complete their agendas satisfactorily. While they count on people's support to accomplish their goals, the demands of people, which governments believe can be very unfair, have been worsening government's problems.

On the other hand, people are depending more on success of governments for their own success, which is reasonable except that people are losing their self-drive and stamina. This seems to be in part driven by governments' strategy of making people more engaged in political matters. And things are turning out not quite as expected on both sides. The reality is that governments must govern and people must live and make their dreams come true.

Governments have to do what they have to do even if their activities are bullied by people; we the people need to be more in charge of our own destinies and demand less from governments and more from ourselves. We ought to work on our projects counting on our powers alone before we accept the help of the government. The fast pace of life does not give us the luxury of waiting for those who are more powerful or know better. Besides, with governments, everything takes forever. Don't wait for governments to fix the roads in your town so you can get smooth rides; get a better suspension for your car. In case you can't do that, take the reality for what it is and move on to better your situation by yourself.

When your desires conflict with laws, rules, and regulations, don't spend the rest of your life fighting them. Find other ways to get what you need and want. Rely on other sources if that's a must. Part of relying on your own powers to achieve your goals includes greater participation in and attention to your projects and less involvement in political matters unless the political road is your way to excellence.

It's much easier and more fruitful to give your contributions to the success of your government through your empowerment than all other means. Say you became a billionaire; your taxes alone are a great contribution to the success of your government. On the contrary, the longer you fight the government on issues that stand in your way and the more ferociously you push for governments' attention to your demands, the longer it will take for your dreams to come true.

Cooperation between governments and people grew sour long ago with no sign of reconciliation in sight, but with or without you, governments have their feet embedded in solid ground. What about you?

Be glad if your government has its feet embedded in solid ground. People can take one government down but then replace it with another government; governments will never disappear. You can be sure that the relationship between governments and people will always be antagonistic. People can't control governments' agendas or force governments to do what they promised to do and should do. Governments will never fully satisfy people's wishes, desires, and demands. With or without you, your government is progressing strongly while you're limping. Give Caesar what's Caesar's and keep what's yours.

The time you waste pointing fingers and cussing out governments for your misfortune could be spent on empowering yourself. When you allow an entity or individual to run your show, you can count on nasty surprises or poor performance. You can be in charge of your destiny with what governments have available for you free or for sale. And then like a miracle, you'll love governments and governments will love you almost unconditionally. Or if they don't, at least you'll never be brokenhearted.

Reading between the lines and filling in the blanks are your only unbreakable tools to help you understand governments and fix the sections of your life broken by governments.

6

Friends and Friendships

Wouldn't it be nice if some things never got sick or died? Life would for sure be way more interesting, less frightening, and full of love, peace, brotherhood, and harmony. I believe it would be nice, but this is nothing more than wishful thinking.

We have yet to understand the reasons behind the death of all realities—and yes, that includes the universes with the creatures and everything in them. We cry when our pets, idols, friends, relatives, and parents die, and we're devastated when our children die. The first reason for our anguish and emotional pain is that we know once a creature is gone, it's gone forever, and we don't have certainty of an afterlife.

When friends and friendships are no more, we are in distress. The time required to recuperate from this emotional state is directly proportional to the length and deepness of the love, care, and nurture given and received. Friends and friendships are deservedly important.

Friends' and friendships' deaths have two stages, one hypothetical and one real. We can be emotionally affected when our true friends and acquaintances become strangers, and we can be as emotionally affected when they die. The desire for friends and friendships is innate; we act on it instinctively during our ages of innocence. And in adulthood, friends and friendships can be born out of convenience.

We made friends even before we understood what friends were. In kindergarten, we had plenty of friends; during our teen years, we had many more. And later, our friendships are like ketchup and french fries, peanut butter and jelly, cream and coffee. Our interactions with our friends benefit us in many ways. Friends are a must-have for normal development; without them, there would be a gap in our personality development reflected in poor social behavior.

During adulthood, we don't care much about making friends or creating friendships instinctively. Bias, prejudice, and misconceptions interfere in the arenas of friends and friendships. We become selective, and personal gain is what triggers it. We're more likely to become friends with schoolmates who can give us a helping hand with homework and hints about dating and sexual matters. We'll become friends with the friends of those we're interested in dating. At work, we'll make friends with those who can help us get ahead there. This strategy is at work in many areas of life. Life without friends is in many ways empty.

So why do we neglect friendships and die friendless? We don't. This river takes its own course. Once we hit age thirty-five, friendships take a nosedive, and we leave friends behind in two ways: the friendship has fewer friends and the remaining friends haven't much friendship. Here's why.

After age thirty-five—earlier for some and later for others—is the time to take the bull by the horns. Goodbye to nightclubs and sleeping over at a friend's house to meet boys and girls. On top of that, many friends have moved away and we've lost contact with them. By that time, we have also dropped friendships that were not that strong to begin with. The irony of life has hit.

As if this is not bad enough, the few friends we have left—usually our best friends—are no longer capable of keeping the character they held before or are unable to meet our expectations. As much as we all want to be best friends forever, life's responsibilities—family, employment, aging parents, marriages, and second marriages among many other things—make it impossible for friends to be there when they're needed the most. There's a reduction in activities that friends can do together as well as less time to do them. This friendship auto dive leaves friends with an unappreciative feeling and waking up far from sight thus far from mind. At old age, this sentiment is painful and heartbreaking and yet is almost a one-size-fits-all phenomenon.

Once, a ninety-year-old veteran told me he couldn't wait to die. He'd been going for regular walks, taking care of small house repairs, and doing light yard work. He was very fit for his age. So I asked him the reasons for his dissatisfaction, and he said, "I'm lonely. All my friends are dead."

Unfortunately, there's not much we can do to change the fate of friends falling into friendship only and then friendship death, but we can minimize the damage it causes. We must respect the dynamics of friendship and reduce our expectations of them.

Fake Friends

We can make many fake friends simply by going on Facebook and sending someone a friend request. At times, jerks or pretty girls in a bad mood respond with, "Do I know you?" Usually, we ignore them if they give us such a heads-up about the kind of friends they would be. For the most part, people know we're simply looking for increasing the number of online friends to show off or for business purposes, so they accept all friend requests. From here, we check the profile in detail to learn as much as we can from what we're looking at and reading as the first steps toward turning online friendships into real friendships. In some cases, online friendships become real friendships involving partying behind closed doors all the way to a ring on the finger. If only that happened more often! The reason it doesn't is that online friends are, well, online friends. Fake friends. But online friends aren't so damaging to our world of friendship. We know beforehand that such friends are fake, and we hope to turn some of them into real friends. This attitude keeps us safe from harm caused by fake friends. Even if we end up hurt, we won't be devastated.

In contrast, the betrayal of friends whom we had trusted can kill friendships and destroy our trust. The tragedy is that real friends who can turn into fake friends are always among us and aren't easy to identify. They eventually trip, and their true characters are revealed. Nevertheless, we should be on the lookout for fake friends lurking in our friendship campus, stay calm, and back off or end the relationship at the first sign of fake friendship.

Saving Private John Doe

On our journeys, each curve contains things we have to clean up or care for that make us leave our friends behind. The greater our forward walk is, the stronger the forces impeding us from contributing to our friendships are. To make matters worse, the more friends we have, the harder it becomes to maintain a desired friendship. This is disastrous and is crying for our attention to save our friends and ourselves from falling into the friendship-only category.

We can shift our behavior so we can benefit from situations we cannot change. We might not be able to stop friendships from declining, but we can communicate with friends frequently and share our struggles, goals, wishes, and desires, give without expecting to receive, understand the decline of friendships, and be there for our friends when least expected. This behavior maintains friendships.

Do your part to keep your friends friends, but lower your expectations. Despite your best efforts, only your best friends will stay forever. You might die friendless not by your fault; your friends might predecease you. Either way, don't let the sour cream of friends and friendships spoil your coffee. You can walk alone and die happy.

Lately, middle-aged men have become victims of the friendless syndrome. If you're one of them or on the way to becoming one, you have some work to do and no time to waste. Embolden yourself to live friendless without significant disruption to your life. Start making friends today as this happens to be something you can do at any age; it doesn't require heavy lifting or running long distances. This is the approach I recommend because it's easier and brings greater benefits than living friendless does.

7

Society

Society is a beautiful phenomenon. All its purposes fit the cause perfectly. The great life we cherish in amazement and glory is due to our combined forces coming up with the best ways to become happy and successful. As we grow, we look for inspiration to conquer new dimensions and accomplish more than we have.

Sometimes, it looks that we've grown too large, gone too far, and caused enough trouble and that the time to rest is now, but we can't; rest is not part of the human quest. Supposedly, by 2050, there will be more than 10 billion people on the planet. Only God knows how far along we'll be then on the human quest.

Ever wonder why we went to space and the moon and are trying to conquer universes? We have become creatures on the move always chasing bigger, better, and greater.

Exodus

Migration is a defining humankind phenomenon. Whether it's been triggered by need, curiosity, pleasure, or adventure, it's become a need more than anything else. And by the looks of it, it'll remain a need for a long time if not forever.

Unfortunately, it has caused trouble for nationals and immigrants alike. Nationals who feel disempowered by the flow of people are angry at immigrants and particularly the illegals. If you share this sentiment, righteously or not, you might want to spend some time reading between the lines and filling in the blanks, which will allow you to understand that the flow of people—legally as well as illegally—among nations will never end. Here are some supporting facts.

No nation can stand alone to defend itself all the way. No nation has all the talent it needs for economic, scientific, and technological progress. No nation can rule over all nations. Part of friendship agreements among nations includes immigration quotas, but when a government slams a door shut to immigration, it opens windows and back doors.

The unfortunates have gone to extremes to better support themselves and their families, and rich, prosperous nations are their first choices in terms of destination. There will always be rich and poor countries despite the increase of prosperity worldwide.

Manufacturers and farmers benefit from immigration; they rely on cheap but productive laborers. Immigrants work crazy hours (once called Mexican hours) and do so under conditions nationals don't want to face—and shouldn't.

The scarcity of immigrants would reduce the labor force and thus trigger increases in the cost of goods and services, a shortage of agricultural products, and an increase in the need for farming subsidies that reduces funds for social service programs and leaves local, state, and federal projects poorly funded. Many countries are prosperous thanks to the blood, sweat, and tears of immigrants; the US is one proud example of this.

Nations have the moral duty to ease the pain and suffering of immigrants who have been in those countries for years illegally. This moral obligation is echoed by nationals and others who support the documentation of illegals and wisely believe that well-educated immigrants could become valuable contributors to society. In general, they would be producing more and paying taxes as they pursued the American Dream.

Seeing immigrants this way would definitely ease the pain of nationals or anyone hating immigrants. All governments should do a better job of ensuring prosperity for nationals and all immigrants with particular priority to nationals.

A Mixed Team

The dynamic of our crazy, chaotic society could force you to ask, "Can I have it my way?" And the answers would be, "Yes and no."

Many factors impede societies from becoming paradises. First, the constant change of realities kills the possibilities of living in paradise day in and day out. Second, we're equal but not the same. We have the same basic needs but different wishes and desires, which makes the definition of our paradise different from that of others.

Just because you have enough money doesn't mean you can live wherever you want. There's zoning to stop you if your desire interferes with the safety of others or creates problems for the governments; you'll not be granted a construction permit.

The moment you start enjoying some quiet and quality time in your house, your neighbor's loud music, the sputtering of a Honda Civic whose exhaust system is shot or has been modified to be loud, sirens, a domestic tragedy the next street over, gang shootouts, or police chases will end your moments of peace.

You share a crowded world with laws, rules, and regulations everybody must follow.

And the big one is that your freedom ends where the freedom of others begins.

Therefore, it's fair to say that you can't have it your way. Or can you? If you're seriously committed to having it your way, there's a way. It could take lots of headaches, sweat, and desperation, but your determination to take only yes for an answer can push you to find ways to materialize your dreams. You can make your freedom and that of others intertwine without causing problems. If there's a limit on how many oranges you can buy at one store, go to another for the oranges you still need. If you can't build here, build there. If you can't be married in this church by this priest, you can be married at a similar church by another priest.

To have it your way in a crowded space—big or small—you have to sacrifice to endure, but your ability to overcome obstacles can be greater than the resistance you face.

Groups and Classes

Far from the tree. We understand how we evolved and how others will evolve from that white liquid to become geniuses or despicable devils. Many of us simply landed farther from the tree than others have; we've become a society of brothers and sisters with distinctive characters and characteristics, but we have to learn to live with that together.

Personality blend. Society's like a fishing net that scoops up fish, but there's never a perfect catch, and even a good catch can come with disappointments. Fishermen learn to accept what they caught instead of what they wished for. While fishermen can dump unwanted catch back in the ocean, society must accept all personalities. We continue to bury our children, loved ones, parents, strangers, and victims of atrocities committed by individuals suffering from schizophrenia and other mental disorders.

The extremist. Small-time crime and organized crime terrorize society. Its dominant role is part of what defines us. We hold it dear to our hearts and fight for it. Sometimes, we take this attitude too far and travel down troublesome roads. We misinterpret scriptures (or pretend we do), we are brainwashed (or pretend we are), or we simply want to prove a point by committing barbaric acts. Not to say these are the only reasons someone becomes an extremist whether or not understood by society.

Fortunately, society on its journey to honor peace, brotherhood, and justice has been unforgiving of those who try to impose their extreme views on society. Slavery, racism, white supremacy, discrimination, and gender unfairness among other social injustices are facing slow deaths. Social peace and brotherhood have become undefeated. Join them and survive! Let go of what you must, and collect fruit from new trees as you walk your new path. Adjust the flow of thoughts and streamline your river before you go in for a deadly catch.

Where the sun never shines. If you lived in a forest, you'd benefit from green, wild foods, chatting birds, and purified air. You'd be celebrating life in its most beautiful ways in a world absolutely apart from the rest of the world. You'd smile and laugh because all your worries would be vanquished by your amazing surroundings. At night, toads, frogs, and crickets would serenade you to sleep. Your only concerns would be a lack of exposure to the sun and a resulting lack of vitamin D. We may have made a mistake when we emigrated thousands and thousands of years ago from African jungles though I believe it was meant to be so from the beginning. Where the sun never shines is a different paradise, a desert we despise.

In stores, we see people buying foods we don't believe they eat with cards that have our money. We know they're going home to drink, smoke, and have sex like rabbits. They go to bed and wake up whenever they wish. We pay for our groceries with our hard-earned money. We go home to prepare dinner, prepare lunch for the kids the next day, and put them to bed hoping we'll have some energy left to please our partners. We wake up to the buzzing of alarm clocks to get ready for another day of work.

As we wait in the emergency room, a drunk brother with a bleeding nose and life-threatening stab wounds arrives. The staff rushes to save his life while we're waiting and waiting and waiting some more. A helicopter takes him to a hospital better suited for his condition while we're still waiting and waiting. Six months later, he's returned home to find his kids in foster care while the mother is in rehab free of charge because she'd stabbed him in self-defense.

Everywhere we go, we see our sisters and brothers getting care that we pay for. They do wrong but are let go with minor if any punishment. We go through hell to walk straight, but if we slip, we're punished harshly. We cannot resist cussing. And up to now, we haven't seen any lack of sunshine on our sisters' and brothers' desert; we've seen the opposite.

Well, we haven't because we've not read between the lines or bothered filling in the blanks. Had we done that, we would've understood that reality is hell, not paradise. Usually, people getting the most assistance from the government are impoverished. It doesn't matter how sunny a day it is; the sun won't reach their surroundings, let alone their ground, because they're surrounded by quicksand, wolves, and vicious dogs and beasts. They dance with daily frustration, anger, and depression.

At age twenty-five, they have three kids by three fathers. They've already lost most of their front teeth to sugary drinks, junk food, smoking, meth, lack of money for dental care, and careless dental hygiene. All of the above has taken out all beauty from their faces, and their lungs are always screaming for oxygen. They shout at their kids every minute and hurt them about 3 million times in 365 days. The short, happy moments are brought to them by weed, cigarettes, drugs, alcohol, and casual sex (or lots of poor-quality sex). They live where governments choose for them to live. They get what governments allow—the minimum for their survival and the survival of their kids. And yet governments cannot come up with a good plan to stop the very children they provide for from going hungry and thirsty every last week of the month before the assistance check comes in.

There's no room for sunshine on the land of a twenty-seven-year-old with five kids by three moms. He faces the government's hunting him down for child support and has been shot at with bullets of threats, retaliation, and revenge from his children's mothers.

You'd better believe residents of that land walk through valleys of death into deeper abysses every day. They live a life yet to be called a life. And yet they're our brothers and sisters raising our nieces and nephews. We, the lucky ones, need to read between the lines harder and fill in the blanks more thoroughly and then thank the Lord for the strength and courage he gives us during our daily struggles; we should show gratitude for having lives we can improve. We should have compassion for those we may despise for looking lazy and despicable. That would make us feel good and blessed.

Dear residents of the land where the sun never shines, you might be desperate and fed up with your hopeless lives. The shadows of death have nailed you to the cross, and the flames of hell have a lock on you. You're a sacrifice to the gods. But you're not dead. If you are, you can still resuscitate.

You can still gain or regain dignity, be productive, and contribute to society. If there's a will, there's a way.

Where the sun shines partly. The middle class has been seeing sunshine blocked by dark clouds that lately have been hanging around longer. That makes the sacrifice harder and gives madness an opportunity to settle in. The reasons are countless—from global economic chaos to the games being played behind the scenes.

If you want more sunshine, you'll have to push the clouds out of the way yourself. Putting your faith in the government or miracles to shift the dynamics of society to serve the middle class better is a foolish move. Sorry to say, that paradise is no longer coming. If you want it, you'll have to get it yourself in spite of natural disasters, globalization, immigration, corruption, racism, terrorism, betrayal, unfaithfulness, and the pull from the poor and the pushback from the rich.

If you don't want to fall into poverty, get your game going. Empower yourself continuously, and boost your ability to stay ahead of the game. The real action takes place in the gray area and behind the scenes, not in black and white or on stage. That shouldn't surprise you unless you've not been reading between the lines and filling in the blanks. Live your reality instead of struggling in it. You have enough mental resources at your disposal for any project you want to tackle. Each day, things can be harder to handle, but I'm sure you didn't drop yourself in middle-class land overnight or by a miracle. You endured hard work, pain, and sacrifice to get there.

Advance; to allow yourself to fall into the land where the sun never shines is suicidal. To stay in the land of partly sunshine and settling just for what it gives you is about as suicidal because you're moving two steps forward but then five backward—the true reason you feel betrayed by life.

For better or worse, the middle class continues to be the best social class; excitement lives there. If you're not feeling it, you've work to do and you shouldn't wait to do it. Your success reflects on the success of society more than you think. Be an inspiration for the two lands you support—the land where the sun never shines and the land where the sun shines every day. They both depend on you.

Where the sun shines every day. It's true and false that the sun never stops shining on the land of the rich. Sure, they do better than everybody else because money makes money and can make just about any of their dreams come true. They have more than enough and should give more to society, but their desire to get the next better thing and their fear of losing their wealth won't allow it. And so the two monsters—greed and social status—push the wealthy to cut corners and commit despicable acts with bad consequences for the entire society including themselves. Clearly, the sun doesn't shine every day in the land of the rich. That paradise can be tricky; a monster cloud could come out of nowhere and block the sunshine for eternity.

We've learned from the scandals involving rich, famous people and especially politicians, coaches, CEOs, and heads of universities that behind a fortune lie big crimes. Same goes for some big corporations and car manufacturers guilty of fraudulent behavior and criminal actions to increase their profits. Where's the beef? The beef is people enraged by the despicable acts of some members of society. The beef's in the fact that we all should let honesty reign for the good of society. Personal integrity keeps our feet on solid ground while shame drops us from grace like a pumpkin.

See No Evil through the Devil's Eyes

We like to look at history, compare it with the current times, and quickly blame the current times for everything wrong with society. We forget that evolution didn't bring just good and better to society. Comparing the number of deaths caused by human ignorance and stupidity such as wars, terrorism, and crime of all types then and now, we can see that though today's numbers are greater, violence and crime have decreased taking into consideration the population increase. Considering the potential for crime, we've changed from vicious animals into adorable pets! When we forget who we are and go wild on our despicable acts, we bring death and destruction as well as new ways to ensure others' safety and prosperity.

The attacks of 9/11 took more than three thousand lives and brought the world's economy close to its knees. Billions have been spent on anti-terrorism measures, which is still going on, but the world became a much safer place. Each new terrorist act opens new security and safety doors, and the world has become even more united and committed to defeating evil.

It comes down to this: those we despise the most have given us the most. Criminals, terrorists, and evildoers make our lives safer as we stop their plotting. Our unfaithful partners who left us for someone else taught us valuable relationship lessons; the two-faced friends who stabbed us in the back have made us choose friends more carefully before we trust them. They have prepared us to recognize evil people. We can't eradicate social atrocities, but we can learn new tricks to stay safe and progress.

Don't let anything stand in the way of your success. Fear nothing, be confident that you won't be paralyzed by events of the world, and don't see evil through evil's eyes. The evils of society might pause your advancement but will never stop you unless you allow it to. Empower yourself to watch the action behind the scenes, where devilish plans are made. Once you know the enemy's plan, victory is within arm's reach.

Not Seen, but It's There

We've become attached to and dependent on things we could do without—expensive cars, the biggest and best looking house in the neighborhood, yachts, private jets and helicopters, and even islands. This cancerous attitude has spread from individuals to groups and even nations.

China, Russia, India, North Korea, and many other countries go over and beyond to show visitors the wonders they have created, but in reality, such wonders are paradises built on soft land and surrounded by fantasies. Their populations suffer from a lack of basic needs, but they still build breathtaking skyscrapers. Getting to know the regular people in those countries will give you a different picture, not the beautiful picture in front of your eyes.

Russia spent a ridiculous amount of money to host the 2014 Winter Olympics, and Brazil did the same for the 2014 FIFA World Cup as testimonies to their economic prowess, but those shiny castles were built on sand and with soft bricks. Soon after the games, both countries fell into socioeconomic chaos due to the financial burden of the games and other factors such as corruption. When you read between the lines and fill in the blanks, you'll see that perhaps your country is not as dysfunctional as you might have thought and that it's doing better than many other countries.

Don't be fooled by glorifying others' worlds in your mind. A wise man knows that behind every fortune might be a crime. Extend your view to get an accurate picture of all social realities. Collect the good apples from the social tree, avoid the rotten ones, and be wary of those you don't see. Thoroughly wash what you pick before you bite into them.

Individual Empowerment for the Common Good

We're one colossal team. Not all players will be leaders or MVPs. Since a team's success depends on each player individually and collectively, we must bring out our best if we want to go undefeated. We must find a field position that best suits our abilities. It's sad that society has made it impossible for its members to show what they have under their sleeves and in their souls. Education and employment, for example, are the two most important ingredients in a delicious society. Ironically, each day presents harder obstacles for these ingredients to overcome. Society is witnessing social classes drifting away from each other, a phenomenon so transparent that the haves are having too much and the haves-not aren't getting anything significant let alone anything that would empower them.

Everyone is responsible for giving his or her best to society and accepting any and all challenges on the way to making dreams come true. We should all take ourselves where we want to be by accepting nothing less than victory. If we are not progressing, we should not pack our bags and go home. Society needs us all.

We can bring out the best in us for our success and that of our brothers and sisters. We can't all be billionaires and great minds, but we can all contribute to the betterment of society. We can do our part by empowering ourselves to aim high and then worry not; the rest will find their way to the benefit of all. This land is ours, and when we care for our land, the whole property benefits.

What We Had, Have, and Leave

Society is an extension of friendship we created in African jungles millions of years ago. It didn't have much diversity or complexity, so it was well balanced. We evolved, grew, and expanded to the point that we took in the tall, short, big, small, black, white, yellow, green, purple, red, indigenous, citizens, nationals, and immigrants (legal and illegal), geniuses, the well educated, the poorly educated, and the illiterate, the wealthy, rich, poor, and destitute, the religious, atheists, and those not sure, the loving peacekeepers and rebellious terrorists, creators and destroyers—everyone crafted by different hands of experience with gods, aliens, and ghosts to join the party too. We poured all these ingredients into a giant pot that's cooking a deliciously unique meal—society. There's no way we could've created a dish different from what we have or escaped racism, bias, prejudice, hate, cheating, unfaithfulness, barbarity, and all other social phenomena that bring us lots of headaches.

The population increase, ecologically changing conditions, and human beings' desire to break things to create better things have brought us the worst in humankind as well as paradises that have helped us achieve a great deal. At times, we wished we weren't part of this huge, crazy team. Fortunately, it got too late to go home.

Society is something special because we're special. We're the chosen brothers and sisters bonded by equality and difference, justice and unfairness. We keep our differences, squeeze in, and become part of this greatness. And we can make it better. We can take control of our lives, stay ahead of the game, and contribute naturally. And then, we can be proud to have contributed to the society that was handed to us.

We built society, and then we created laws, rules, and regulations for an orderly and prosperous society. Smart moves, but we seem to have a bond with evil. We're constantly looking for opportunities to advance and leave others behind. This devilish trait is the main reason for the social chaos we face. It has not brought peace, stability, happiness, or prosperity to society. The small elite running the show has been corrupted by the desire for the power to twist society to their advantage. They create games too complicated for us to understand, and when we ask for clarification, we learn that twisted minds can't give straight answers, and the gray area is shielded from ordinary minds.

When we read gray areas by ourselves and demand explanations, they apologize for their (false) mistakes. To stay ahead of the game, we can no longer conform with what we've seen, heard, and been told without reading between the lines and filling in the blanks. That allows us to understand that the whole is the sum of its parts and to realize that embracing black and white blindfolds us to society's dynamic, which can be seen and experienced only in the gray area.

Contrary to what's being sold to us, society is not there to build our castles; we have to build them ourselves. We can cry as much as we want for a society filled with peace, love, care, and brotherhood that pleases and benefits all its members without discrimination, bias, or prejudice, but that society hasn't arrived yet, and it won't ever arrive. If it ever does, you can be sure it shouldn't be called society.

Use what you have to get what you want instead of being paralyzed waiting for what you need. Live, and let die what must die. Do your best to achieve your goals with grit, integrity, and honesty while accepting society with its diversified groups and classes.

The blueprint of the society of the future depicts humans, robots, and artificial intelligence sharing a highly cooperative society—We hope. We keep our fingers crossed that robots and artificial intelligence don't turn into disobedient smart creatures pushing their creators back to caves on Mars. In the meantime, let's not mourn the past or worry about what we'll leave for others. Instead, let's focus on becoming an excellent society with what we have now.

When we work hard and see ourselves going nowhere fast while others sip gold and spit silver, we must realize that what we can contribute to the whole makes humankind flourish. Don't feel trapped by those above you or feel you're a king lording it over those below you. Someone might always have a better meal than you do, but that shouldn't stop you from enjoying what's on your plate. There will always be people prettier, smarter, and richer than you, but you can stay truthful to your goals and stand your ground with dignity and respect for the benefit of society.

8

Why Gender Equality?

LIFE WOULD BE A WONDERFUL adventure if males didn't feel the need to maintain their dominance and other genders didn't have to put up with disrespect and abuse and being treated as objects for males' satisfaction. Homosexuals, lesbians, bisexuals, and transgenders should be living without fear of governmental persecution and society's hatred rooted in bias, prejudice, and the refusal to accept others for who they are. Society and happiness would blend into one big perfect picture with gender equality. And since we've seen what world delivers to gender equality, picture perfect is what we should fight for until we get it.

Wouldn't it be a bit of a stretch to embark on a daunting and chaotic quest for gender equality? Are we saying what we mean and meaning what we're saying or simply throwing ourselves into battlefields without knowing what we want to accomplish? I think we might be ignoring some important voices here.

The Voices of Mysteries

As far as we know, the big bang was heard 14 billion years ago. Its echo gave us the universes and all creatures and things. We all share the beautiful, starry skies, and some parts down here on earth are rich in natural resources, but the majority of land contains little or no treasures. Water, vegetation, animals, and climate are distributed unevenly and unequally around the globe.

In every aspect of life and environment, we find differences. We human beings are different in the ways we walk, speak, interact, compete, cooperate, exhibit intellect and beauty, eat, drink, sleep, and have sex. We are equal but not the same. Twins go their different ways, and few families have more than one or two movie stars, doctors, lawyers, professors, and so on.

In matters involving gender, differences are there. When they become parents, men and women alike release oxytocin, the love hormone, but it affects them differently. Oxytocin drives women to nurture and affection and men to protect and defend. God created women as beautiful, loving, and caring creations and men as beasts, jackasses, and protectors. Biology also tells us that men and women process hormones, medication, and a ton of things differently, a phenomenon scientists can't explain. We know that women behind the wheel of school buses feel a lot of responsibility in their hands while fighter pilots in cockpits feel in charge of something awesome.

You can cry to divinity and humanity as much as you want, but neither will give you what you're asking for—death of gender inequality and vigor equality. Equality has never been the name of the game. There's no God, big bang, government, friends, beasts, or anything to allow it to be. That makes your crying for equality foolish. On the other hand, inequality is a necessary element that balances universes, humanity, and realities within. I've heard so many people including women saying that fighting for gender equality is nonsense. They'd be winners is my court if I had one. For all obvious reasons, you don't have my shoulders for your crying for gender equality. You do have my unconditional support with love and devotion with your fighting for justice and fairness for all genders. That's just and fair. And yet, is this fight reasonable or insanity? Let's dig into that.

Injustice and Unfairness

Some things are what they are. We ought to accept them and choose a course of action that benefits us. Those whose names are in the Guinness World Records book have power and talent ordinary people don't and can't match. Female stars and superstars are talented and beautified head to toe. They have the looks—heads full of long, thick hair, beautiful faces, kissable lips, amazing noses, beautiful eyes, perfect breasts that draw males' attention, and slender bodies that make men eat their hearts out. They carry great melodies in their souls, and their hearts are full of love and compassion.

Some of us are born with golden spoons in our mouths while others have to do with wooden spoons. We save those who want to die and let those who deserve to live die of pain, anguish, and misery. The police kill the very people they protect, and people kill police, their protectors and servants. We humans destroy the habitats of other animals for our benefit. Isn't that enough injustice and unfairness? But there's more.

In some countries, people can be jailed for animal cruelty and for urinating in the bushes while in other countries such as India, police ignored the rights of a woman who was raped to press charges under the pretext that she had brought on being raped. In many places, men can have many wives, while women, on top of being victims of arranged marriages, can be stoned to death for infidelity.

Since 1998, abortion under all circumstances has been illegal in El Salvador. As a result, dozens of women have been imprisoned for having abortions that the state considered homicides. Alba Lorena Rodriguez received a thirty-year sentence for homicide after a miscarriage that the state blamed her for provoking. Police frame suspects and send juveniles to prison for political and economic gain. The skin color, ethnicity, and families of accused people as well as the mood of a judge (based on whether he or she had sex the previous night or what he or she had for breakfast) can influence the outcome of a trial. Nations spend billions to acquire nuclear weapons while ordinary people suffer from hunger, starvation, and oppression.

Even if we're not fine with all that, we must shrug our shoulders and move on with our lives. We know that injustice and unfairness are shameful, but we choose to be unjust and unfair. We are surrounded by injustice and unfairness, which seem ingrained in society. Then fighting for gender justice and fairness is a joke. Except it's not, especially now that we're living in an era when females are ascending and males are descending in terms of superiority. (It's about time, ladies!)

Females Rise and Male Supremacy Declines

Those in doubt about female dominance being on the horizon are not being truthful about the gender social shift. There's been a steady increase in the number of women pursuing careers once deemed to be the domain only of men. Hilary Clinton was as close as it could get to becoming the first female president.

Fed up with oppression, disrespect, and restraints, women are fighting for their right to equal pay and equal job opportunities. They're spitting on taboos, biases, and prejudices and gaining economic independence. Social changes such as same-sex marriage, online dating, relationships of convenience, and open marriages and relationships are allowing women to live as they want without the penises or helping hands of men. Even in oppressive countries, female voices are becoming louder and are being listened to and taken more seriously.

Females are becoming more determined to gain higher education while males aren't even waking up to the fact that females are empowering themselves socially and economically and not worried about getting a ring from the best suitors. They can live single happily forever. Guys will end up as girls' cooks, butlers, and secretaries. If men can't see this coming, the problem is theirs; they'll watch women climb and dominate. (I love it!) They better accept and face the truth—females will get their fair share no matter the efforts and tricks of men to stop them from advancing.

The fight for justice and gender fairness is a reasonable fight that must go on despite the fact that women will face strong resistance; determination will help them overcome that.

Who Are the Enemies?

On the battlefields of gender justice and fairness, there are more enemies of different forms, sizes, and shapes than you can imagine, ladies. Here are some.

Biology. If we take three-year-old boys and girls to a toy store, the boys will go for cars, balls, building materials, ninjas, soldiers, and other toys that display action, power, and violence while girls will go for dolls and dollhouses.

Supremacy. If Johnny can't get it up, there's no party, while girls don't need to feel aroused in order to have sex. A penis is a weapon. A vagina can't hurt a man. (We'd love watching you try, ladies!) Men are sperm sprayers—the pitchers. Women are babymakers—the catchers. Men never expect flowers, and when they receive jewelry, they feel rewarded for a job well done. When women receive flowers and jewelry, they feel loved and appreciated.

Strength. As far as strength goes in general, a female is no match for a male. Men handle carpentry, plumbing, mowing the lawn, and cleaning the pool while women clean the house, cook, and so on. Women might fight on the front lines, but they'd be better nurses than men.

Like attracts like. Boys hang out with boys and talk about how many girls they will sleep with. Girls get together to talk about beauty, family, and why boys are such idiots who never get it. These biological forces are strongly wired and thus hard to defeat.

External factors. Many became misogynists who believe that women are inferior to men in all ways and find fuel for their idiocy in taboos, culture, tradition, and other philosophical principles preaching as following.

Love, respect and protect. We grow up to love Mommy and respect Daddy. "You never hit a girl" is the law in homes that is reinforced by the laws of the land for boys to follow.

Ideology. A mother should nurture the family while a father must provide for it; girls must take good care of their skin and their public image and be nice, humble, submissive, and feminine in order to get good husbands. Boys must be raised to be soldiers and girls must be princesses. Hard labor is for men, and secretarial jobs are for women. Men become surgeons while women become nurses. When women are in charge of complicated tasks such as flying, the world expects a lower outcome in case of emergencies. "You throw like a girl!" are humiliating words boys tell girls.

Hidden factors. Equal pay, men believe, would open the doors for a decline in family values. This philosophy has been knocked down by laws in many countries and has given way to the concept of equal pay for equal work; thus, men look for opportunities to give women a sucker punch.

Females could be denied upper-management positions under the pretext that the job requires lots of traveling with overnights. Suddenly, reliability becomes the number one requirement for job qualification just to make it harder for women to apply. In many workplaces, sexual harassment and the derogatory treatment of women are strategies to discourage females from self-empowerment.

All the above are harsh, heartless, and unfair, but queen bees salt the wounds as females in power do not open doors for other females. The condescending attitude toward women are a stronghold for companies to pay women less than they do men and justification for their refusing to accept women for certain types of work.

Fight Smarter, Not Harder

Learn as much as you can about all fighting instruments at your disposal—biological and man-made—as well as the best times to use them. Stay vigilant to the aces your opponents will play. When they're laid on the table, let them roll; just plan your moves. Don't rely on gender justice and fairness as your strongest soldiers, and don't spend the rest of your life protesting gender injustice. Don't waste your time proving that gender justice and fairness are protected by the Constitution either. On the contrary, contribute to the cause up to the point of no harm to your advancement, learn as much as you can about the male-dominant world, and find ways to infiltrate that world and its mindset—and victory will be yours.

To fight smarter also means letting men believe you're weaker and inferior and then hitting them with knockout blows. It means getting more with less, gliding to your destination when you run out of fuel, and seeing with your eyes closed. You can make up for not getting a raise by stretching your salary further and being more in charge, more assertive, and happier than your male counterparts who are getting paid more. You can come out a winner when you're cheated on or when the cards are dealt to the benefit of your opponents—the male cheaters.

Every corner of life is filled with injustice and unfairness particularly toward other genders whether you want to call it gender inequality, gender bias, gender prejudice, gender abuse, or gender slavery. What matters is your understanding that men and women are equal but not the same; justice and fairness ought to be served to all genders.

When females fight for gender equality, they're dismissing the fact that they are gold mines while men are nothing more than tools women can use to dig for their treasures. A mother is twice what a father could ever be. It takes a man a few seconds to become a father while it takes a woman nine months to become a mother. Men are stronger, but women are smarter. Women will be bowing to thieves and predators of their supremacy when they cry out for gender equality. Male supremacy is after all a bluff; women know that.

While men were in the jungle hunting, women were keeping their children safe. When men were napping, women were cooking dinner. Women sewed men's clothing for their protection in the jungle. When children got sick, women sent men to the jungle to bring leaves, seeds, and roots so they could make medicines. Women constantly battled on many fronts of life while men were monkeying around in the jungle. Women gained superiority over men by learning to multitask.

Women got the upper hand in problem solving while men were engaged in tasks that would make them Tarzans. Women were doing the thinking while men were doing the doing most of the time under women's supervision. Women were simply exposed to more situations requiring brainpower while men were exposed to more situations requiring strength and survival skills. To this day, women say, "Let's sit down and talk about it" while men say, "Let's go outside and settle it like men."

Evolution molded women to be smarter than men, but men didn't like that, so they began using their strength and louder mouths to confuse women about their superiority. They tried to make women submissive under the false pretense that men's jobs—providing for and ensuring the safety of their families—was more demanding than cooking for the family or raising their children.

When men couldn't provide while claiming that women were asking for too much and should shut up, women had to borrow some meat and honey from neighbors but had to tell men that they had gone to chat about female stuff so their men's egos wouldn't be hurt. When men were pleasuring others and themselves outside home and leaving women at home longing for love, care, and sexual satisfaction, they had to find emotional and sexual balance outside the cave. Upon finding that out, men started calling women liars and cheaters.

How did men make society believe that their sexual satisfaction had to come first? God might've created Eve from Adam's rib, but I'm sure he demanded that Adam satisfy her sexually first, and she rewarded him with their babies.

Biology caught men lying; a clitoris has 8,000 nerve endings while penises have only 4,000. On top of all that, religious organizations—founded and led by men—came in to squeeze people's sexual expression to just about nothing, and they helped leaders enact social laws intended to give men power over women. Despite the fight, women suffered defeat until the sixties, a time when they got fed up with men's abuse, injustice, and unfairness and started the journey toward regaining the power they had had.

Science and biology have proven female supremacy in many areas, and we know that men can lie to themselves and others. A clear example of this is the false notion that blacks are an inferior race, which has been proven wrong by science and biology. The notion that females are emotionally too weak to fight on the front lines doesn't hold water when female soldiers rescue injured male soldiers crying out for their moms (with due respect).

Women fought to keep their supremacy, but men refused to back down; they plotted to keep women from flourishing. And so, men told stories instead of history to future generations. For millions of years, men have been telling society that they are the superior gender.

Men's attempts to subjugate women should motivate women to continue their fight for justice and fairness for all genders forcefully and strategically. Men are always looking for opportunities to screw women and get away with it. Women should be respectful but no more humble than necessary in this battle for what is rightfully theirs. They will need to read between the lines and fill in the blanks in this murky water that men are constantly adding dirt and dust to, but women's intellect, wisdom, and grit make them a superior beast. They should stay the course. Victory is close and smiling at them.

God created Adam. He looked at him and said, "I can do better than that!" He then created Eve.

9

The Globalization Syndrome

THE GOVERNMENT SOLD GLOBALIZATION TO people on the basis of global prosperity, but stress, frustration, and anger were the result. We are far from the promised land; people's lives are in turmoil. The water might be calm, but deep down, it's boiling.

So many nations are mad as hell at China and are experiencing the rage of citizens who are shouting for a game change. Their shouts are prompted by their anger at governments for the status quo and political correctness, hatred for immigrants and Muslims, and a rise in racism, white supremacy, nationalism, and anti-Semitism. And to show they meant business, the British voted to "Brexit," and the Americans elected an eccentric—Donald Trump—for president.

How Did We Get It So Wrong?

When we were teenagers, we did not understand why people acted so stupidly, why the world was crazy and ignorant, the math teacher was so gay, and why our siblings were so annoying. We did not want to hear that we were the problem. We wanted to hear, see, and talk no evil. We simply wanted everybody out of our way so we could live our way.

Well, we aren't teenagers anymore. We no longer let our tempers overshadow our ability to reason. Therefore, with cool heads, let's see why we got globalization so wrong and find ways to repair the damage.

Heart of the Matter

The reasons for the chaos caused by globalization are many including terrorism, China, mistrust and selfishness among nations, corporations, technology, natural disasters, wars and threats of war, the monkey-see-monkey-do syndrome, and Russia.

Terrorism. After the calamities of world wars, we had to come up with a better strategy for peace and unity among nations paying attention in particular to sharing intelligence about terrorists plotting attacks, and that worked for the most part. With terrorism in check, global prosperity became the number two priority. Now more than ever, rich countries cooperate for global prosperity and faster deliveries of its benefits, and they have invited developing countries to join the band.

The World Trade Organization, created in 1995 to promote global prosperity, was helped in achieving its goal by the explosion of technology. And the band was playing a variety of genres to soothe the different souls at the table. Things were going great until 9/11, when the world's economy was knocked out cold. Global security had to be the priority of all priorities. George W. Bush, the president at the time, spent ridiculous amounts of money on security measures both for the US and for other countries. The global economy had been shot in both legs, and the result was a horrible rise in unemployment and other economic pain; the US was sneezing, and the world caught a cold.

China. No nation can control a snake with a thousand heads some of which spit venom. The US, England, France, and other countries wanted to kill China for its currency manipulation, product dumping, and other business practices in violation of the World Trade Organization. The world's been unable to make China play by the rules.

Mistrust and selfishness among nations. Agreements between nations are always violated because despite all the smiles and handshakes, nations do not trust each other. That's simply part of business as usual and the reason trust but verify is every country's policy.

Despite the friendship and the spirit of compromise between some nations, globalization encourages competition. Each nation pulls burning charcoal to the side of grill where their burgers, hot dogs, and chicken thighs are barbecuing. I don't understand how the US, England, and France stayed so behind in this game. I guess cavaliers do fall off their horses more often than we think. Spectators suffer greater pain than fallen riders do.

Corporations. All corporations aim to maximize profits, and globalization offers them greater opportunities to do so. They partied hearty and moved the party when they had had their fill, but they left nothing for the poor. The 1 percent got wealthier, and the 99 percent got poorer. Unfair wealth distribution is the king of all King Kongs in the globalization room, the main cause of our stress, frustration, pain, and misery.

As bad as this is, we shouldn't blame the filthy rich for doing what they do well. While we might be thinking fairness is a moral obligation for everybody, corporations think only of increasing their profits, so they'll take a big bite of our small piece of the pie or even the whole thing. That's what greed drives greedy people to do. I think they know about it and love it with a passion. Globalization has promoted their greed at the expense of others.

Technology. Companies buy machines to get more productivity out of fewer employees. Prioritizing employees who would avoid injuries because they want to stay working with almost a complete disregard for their poor pay and horrendous working conditions is part of the game too; companies adore such loyalty. And then came automation and online businesses and services with their bags of candy and bottles of potion.

Do you remember standing in line in banks on payday to cash your paycheck and wanting to choke the tellers and other customers who were so slow? How about enduring long lines at the post office for a simple book of stamps? Technology fixed those problems. Online banking has been a lifesaver; we can deposit checks, pay creditors, and transfer money while we're cooking dinner. We continue expanding online services but unfortunately at the expanse of job losses. I think that is a small price to pay for all the benefits technology gives us, but the time will come that that small price will become too expensive for the majority of people to pay, and they will blame globalization.

Natural disasters. Natural disasters have increased in size, frequency, and devastation. Every time one occurs, millions of dollars leave the government's coffers. If you don't suffer big losses and your job's still there, you might still suffer the consequences of a natural disaster through a freeze on raises, a reduction in working hours, or layoffs. People on government assistance are usually the first to suffer consequences anytime money leaves the government's coffers, but people in general get mad when that money goes to other countries for dealing with the consequences of natural disasters there. And the blame goes to globalization.

Wars and threats of war. Nothing brings devastation to humanity more than wars. Besides having a direct impact on lives and property, wars make us stay behind the game whoever we are and wherever we are, and it doubles our troubles if we're victims of displacement.

Threats of war bring just about same consequences as wars do. The world is pretty much used to wars of words between nations (Remember the exchange of words between North Korea's leader Kim Jong-un and President Trump?), but it's becoming more serious every year. Whether or not this is all a political game, nations are concerned and people are worried rightfully so because they must be prepared for what could happen, and they focus more on defense instead of economic prosperity, and that holds them back.

The monkey-see-monkey-do syndrome. The world faces a continuous, toxic, and contagious wave of social hatred. Whether this reality is triggered by Russia's attempt to prompt civil wars in rival nations, when you hate people of different colors, races, ethnicities, or backgrounds, you're ingesting bitter pills. Hatred keeps you frustrated and disempowered, unable to reason without prejudice. Your state of spirit and mind pulls you down. Instead of improving yourself, you're cussing people out, wishing they'd evaporate, or plotting something evil. Worse is when your reasons for blaming your troubles on globalization come from fake sources you have been following dearly.

We tend to join crowds that speak our language and say what we want to hear; that's why we're easily fooled by political rhetoric. And that keeps us from seeing that we might've joined a crowd of losers or a club of winners who won't make the cut. Check the water for harmful chemicals and foreign objects before you jump into the pool, and never jump in just because somebody else just did. Monkey see monkey do can bring nasty surprises.

Russia. As globalization was extending the world's unity, peace, and prosperity and more nations rose to power, Russia saw the number of its allies shrinking; it didn't have many cards to play. But Russia, the only superpower that has stood up to American bullying, couldn't bear the shame. Putin, a political genius for better or worse, became Russia's president first in 2000 and ruled until 2008 to put Russia back on its feet, and he did. He came back in 2012. In no time, Russia was walking again. Soon after, it started shouting for attention with its bullying Ukraine in 2014, and the world started paying attention.

Still unhappy, Russia harbored Assad, the president of Syria who was killing civilians who opposed his authoritarian regime. The civil war in Syria—probably all orchestrated by Putin to show the world that Russia was not a fallen superpower but a major player in international affairs—was going to spin the world way more out of control than the rest of the world had predicted. Global democracy and prosperity for all seemed to be only over Putin's dead body. Little by little, he came out of shadows to openly help Assad fight a chaotic war.

Now, the US and Russia are on same battlefield fighting for different sides and exchanging words of caution. And the world, instead of focusing on fixing economic problems created by globalization, is concerned about a war between the two powerful nations. Russia's getting attention and respect from the world, but it wants to dominate the game. Destroying strong bonds among European nations and other Western countries and having their citizens tear each other apart would be a powerful blow to globalization and a jackpot for Russia and Putin. Helping candidates who are sympathetic to Russia to win elections is Russia's secret bargaining chip. According to some reports, more than a dozen European countries suffered from Russia's meddling in their presidential elections. Sadly, the US forgot to wear its special goggles and was tricked by Russia's meddling in the 2016 presidential election. The US is out for revenge, but it's too late; Russia has already thrown its most powerful punch yet at globalization.

While the world has yet to declare Russia the victor, it does have globalization on the ropes, and the world is suffering because of that. Anytime the US and Russia are at odds with each other, the rest of the world worries about the economic consequences.

The foregoing illustrates the reasons you feel screwed by globalization. What you see, read, and hear could be fake information driving you to wrongful reasoning and to blaming the innocent for your stress, frustration, pain, and misery. Globalization is your ally, but in every game, there are winners and losers.

Big Winners, Winners, and Losers

Big winners. Big businesses were the first to ask governments for cooperation expansion among nations—globalization. After 9/11, it was time for a shift in their business strategy. Countries with low labor costs and fewer regulations including China and India were appealing. The top dogs around the world took their top tech-brains to dinner to discuss ways of reducing and substituting for human labor. The meal was delicious. Everybody went home happy especially the big shots who were holding magic cards that would let them win every game. Yes, money talks louder and bullshit walks slower in a bad economy. The magic trick paid off; big corporations grabbed all the cash on the table and built the largest trophy stand imaginable for all their awards.

The next set of big winner's prizes was snatched by nations. Germany took the silver, and China grabbed the gold, and like big corporations, it grabbed all the cash on the table.

Winners. Thanks to globalization, many countries experienced economic growth, happiness, and prosperity. Immigrants saw an opportunity to make their dreams come true. They all won bronze medals. (Contrary to what many believe, immigrants aren't winners; they left their countries because they were losers there. But all things considered, they do better where they land.)

Losers. The losers of globalization are the employees whether they are nationals or immigrants who lose their jobs because they couldn't compete with the higher productivity of and the lower wages accepted by immigrants, big companies increasingly rely on technology for productivity increases and thus reduce the need for human labor, and their jobs have moved overseas or small companies they worked for were bought or crushed by giants—Walmart, Home Depot, Lowe's, Best Buy, and Amazon.

The US, England, France, and their nationals are losers too as well as are Germans, who didn't really lose but were shouting their fear of losing especially when the Christian Democrat Angela Merkel, Germany's first female chancellor, allowed more than a million people from the Middle East, West Asia, and Africa to enter the country and offered asylum to refugees who were fleeing chaos in Syria in 2015. And last but not least, Russia is the loser because it decided to take prizes by force and secretly disrupt the game of globalization. As we learn more each day, Russia did not secretly disrupt globalization; it stepped on the gas and adopted new measures to reach its goals quicker.

Big winners have the brightest smiles while big losers are pissed off. But late is better than never especially when there's a will. If you're a loser in the game of globalization, don't cry over your losses. Read between the lines and fill in the blanks so you can empower yourself and become a winner. Create a strategy to dominate the game, and stay ahead of it.

Winning Strategies

Just as we have, globalization has evolved. It grew when we had families of our own. It grew bigger when we made friends. It grew even bigger when we created tribes and then large communities. It expanded when we created nations. Globalization is one of the greatest steps toward making world a better place for all. This beautiful giant's not going anywhere. Russia and others are trying to knock it down, but it's needed more than ever.

If you can't stand globalization, you're shooting yourself in both feet. This ship, sadly and quite surprisingly, drifted off course and left many in distress and disbelief, but it's a safe ship taking you to your destination. You can't jump off to stop seasickness and madness, nor can you kick everybody out or refuse to share. Going after the captain who sank the ship and cursing others in lifeboats is a fool's move. You have to focus on swimming to shore through rough waters and surviving and then thriving. Figure out what brought you down and then go on stronger; to stick your head in the sand is to expose your buttocks to predators. Once you know what you want, focus on getting it whether the world is your friend or foe.

Worshiping individualism and nationalism in isolation doesn't cut it. Nowadays, if you grab your ball and go home, the game will still go on—everybody has a ball—and you'll be a loser. The US pulled out of the Paris Accord and the Pacific Trade Deal, but others are still playing the game and calling for prosperity for humankind, not just for a nation or two.

It matters not how you see globalization; you're still receiving its benefits. The variety of products available at low prices everywhere give witness to globalization's benefits; the luxury of traveling to just about everywhere does that as well. It could be that you're jobless, divorced, living in the basement of your grandmother's house, or homeless and no longer know how it feels to be happy or have sex all thanks to globalization. You'll look with disdain at your friends and neighbors who are the winners of globalization. Well, you aren't dead yet. Put a strategy to work. Any time you set firm goals and embrace sacrifice, you can become a hero. And the best of all winning strategies is you. The following tips should help.

Be healthy and strong—Eat right, and exercise regularly.

Don't be a follower; be a leader—Empower yourself to read between the lines and fill in the blanks.

Prioritize your financial health.

Quarantine your wants, control your needs, avoid intruders, stick to a budget, and shield yourself from advertisers and hoarding.

Don't go to bed with dogs if you don't want to fight fleas—Your partner can make you or destroy you.

Don't bite off more than you can chew—buying a $70,000 car that keeps you broke is foolish.

Share with tomorrow—The old can be despicable Grinches.

Don't allow any person or reality to dictate your destiny or to become an impossible obstacle. Be confident, focus on your prize, be aware of challenges, and be ready to defeat your enemies.

Don't stay hungry because the kitchen is too hot; open the windows and buy fans.

Obviously, higher education empowers you to do all the above.

We don't have power over globalization, but we must not allow it to ruin our lives. The players behind the scenes are acting for their own benefit, but you don't have to simply watch their play; you can engage in it yourself. Your shouting, "This show sucks!" or set the building on fire will do you no good. Don't be victimized by globalization whether you're for or against it. Instead of fighting it, dance with it all night long and let people watch in disbelief.

10

The Poverty of Poverty

Everyone fought for food and drink. School's a nightmare, and home's hell. Dad always went to his best friend's house or hit the bars for a drink or two to put out the flames of heated arguments he had with Mom. Most of the time, their arguments were about rumors of infidelity, which could've been true as both had to be looking for comfort and stress relief outside marriage.

We grew quickly and were disrespectful. Instead of taking advantage of things that would've helped us get and stay ahead, we were in the streets causing trouble or running for safety. Mom and Dad would repeatedly borrow money to bail us out. At no time did our grandparents take care of us because we were serving time.

Someone who was living on the street asked some friends to beat up his drunken father for having kicked him out of the house. And then he became a father himself. Incapable of being a dad, every now and then, he snuck over to his girlfriend's house more for casual sex than out of love for his children as he believed that the liquor, bags of weed, and $65 entitled him to "some." Such parties relieved his frustration.

But it was Friday the thirteenth. He impregnated her again. He had to hide from the child support authorities. If he managed to land a job, it would be under a fake name, and he'd be paid under the table or see no more than $189 on his weekly paycheck. He hit the streets day and night as the solution for all his problems, and he hoped not to end up shot or dead.

When middle age knocked on the door, nothing had improved, so we stayed hopeless. Our kids had grown up to hate us. As much as that hurt, we weren't good mothers or fathers, a shame we must bear for the rest of our lives. There's not much for them to grab onto and have better luck than we did. We feel sorry for not having provided them a path to success. Like father, like son, and like mother, like daughter had struck again.

I am sure you've heard such a story either from a victimized person or an elderly person who had seen it all. And there you have it: a little taste of the rough, sad, and yet normal life in deep poverty—the poverty of poverty.

Not as draconian but deserving some empathy is some salt to the poverty of poverty wounds. When the poverty of poverty forces people to the hospital usually after symptoms have reached the concerned stage, they don't take medications as prescribed, they don't follow their doctor's recommendations, and they don't change the bad behavior that got them sick in the first place. On top of that, they have bad diets and don't exercise. A sickness they could easily have managed turns into an illness, a blowing wind in an already freezing temperature.

It's a good thing that governments have social services for the poor; that avoids a whole world of extreme chaos, but accepting social services is like accepting a sword that shatters in battle or scuba diving with a leaky oxygen tank. The problems that drive people to social services usually increase, and new ones arrive.

On the other hand, the lack of necessary skills to do better whips people in the poverty of poverty alongside stress, trauma, frustration, depression, and rage, which they breathe day in and day out. If somehow people in the poverty of poverty had a lump sum of money, say from scratch tickets, a lucky poker hand, or a settlement from a car accident, they'd most likely blow it in a week with friends on booze, drugs, and prostitutes.

Those with jobs—usually low-tech jobs—don't earn vacation time, aren't rewarded with raises for hard work and dedication, and don't earn even respect. Within a year or two, they're likely to quit over simple, low-burning flames, be fired due to drug use or some stupid action such as theft, sexual harassment, or disorderly conduct, or for showing disrespect to coworkers and superiors. Their retirement is nothing far from an everyday struggle, which by the way had become their normal. They could have zero communication with their children and no money for their own funerals. People living in the poverty of poverty are winners who didn't make the cut. They spent almost their entire lives where the sun never shined, and they rest under the shadow of death.

Culprits

The poverty of poverty is poverty at its lowest point. It's something the world has ignored either because it was too painful to look at or too complicated to deal with. And that makes everybody as guilty as charged. And then…

The rich and the filthy rich. Rich people understand that it's not a good idea to help the poor excel because the poor are their money generators; the rich supply them with sugary drinks and junk food for almost nothing. (Tons of almost nothing amounts to a gigantic pile of treasure.) The result is health complications. The rich swim in pools of great profit from which they supply the poorest.

Governments. Governments could've done a better job for the poor if they hadn't given so much leeway to the rich. And that partly explains why despite fifty-plus years of fighting poverty in the US, no considerable ground has been gained. With the increasing influence of big money in politics, the poverty of poverty can kiss sunny days goodbye.

Nature. Tornadoes, hurricanes, torrential rains, excessive heat, and other unfriendly weather phenomena leave poor people homeless and with an ocean of problems to solve.

Humans. We're pretty much the sole creator of the poverty of poverty. As we continue our journey of excellence and distinction with 1 percent behind the wheel of prosperity, poverty finds more-suffocating chokeholds, and the poverty of poverty loses hope of coming out of a coma. On top of that, we find ways to be at war every day. Who suffers the most from war? The poor obviously.

Why Should You Care?

John Doe was a twenty-nine-year-old single father of three by different mothers. Poorly educated, he couldn't earn enough to care for himself. Child support cut his paycheck more than in half. He considered it useless to work forty hours a week and take home $193. The streets became irresistible. Dealing drugs is a dangerous business, so John bought guns for protection. A park in town with basketball and tennis courts was a place for him to relieve his stress and frustration and make some cash selling drugs.

Another Friday the thirteenth rubbed salt in his wounds when what he'd bought for protection took the life of an innocent child at the park and landed him jail. The neighborhood was terrified. Parents no longer took their children to that park or any park for that matter. Some residents moved to a safer town, which meant leaving good jobs behind among other losses. Those who owned houses had even worse stress and frustration: "It's much harder now to sell or rent houses here." Authorities stepped up the fight against crime, and it cost them a lot to hire more police.

An increase in crime means that the population will be hit with local, state, and federal taxes and increased fees for public services. Usually, property taxes, car registration, title, and insurance premiums are the first public services to see increases. Businesses are asked to chip in sometimes on top of handling a tax increase. They're also obligated to reinforce security staff and buy surveillance equipment to fight theft. The extra cash to support those costs will come from their consumers. Tourists will end up having a nightmare instead of a relaxing time because their luggage could be stolen or they could be attacked by criminals. The higher the crime rate, the greater the loss of tourism revenue as people go to safer places for vacation.

People like John Doe, who served his time and is out without any golden spoon, are the cause and consequence of the poverty of poverty. The wooden spoon he has is broken. His criminal record made it almost impossible for him to get a job. He owes the government—the taxpayers—$67,189 in child support. He's no longer allowed to leave the state. Before he went to prison, he was in the oven. He's out now and heading to the frying pan. Crime has become his way of life. The only thing he knows how to do well. Or not.

An entire population can suffer the consequences of the poverty of poverty with those living below the poverty line feeling burned. And they're our brothers and sisters. We all should care about these left-behind people. We can try to ease their pain and make sure our families never feel it.

Poverty is a social class, but we shrug in the face of it and go on with our lives. But people in the poverty of poverty didn't just drop themselves in there. I can't find words to describe the shame involved in allowing the poverty of poverty to exist. Simply because the poor will always exist doesn't mean we should add fuel to that fire.

Since the poverty of poverty lacks all the ingredients for a delicious meal, children born into the poverty of poverty inherit bad luck and are born handicapped in many ways. Easing their pain and suffering should be our personal mandate. There are many places we can donate to including the Red Cross, UNICEF, and so on, and even if our contributions are small, they can add up over time. Consider donating as a civic duty fulfilled. Unused power and knowledge don't do anyone any good, and even small acts of heroism are beneficial to all. Caring for those in the poverty of poverty can change our approach to our time (volunteering) and money (donating) management. We can't go wrong by helping our brothers and sisters in need.

Dear residents of the poverty of poverty, as long as you keep on waiting for miracles to give you a helping hand, not much improvement will come your way. While you're keeping your fingers crossed for a president, governor, or some institutional endowment to ease your pain, the clock is ticking and your time is running out. You'll die of misery.

The poverty of poverty seems to be an aggressive social cancer that has killed many and will kill many more if we try to shrug it off. But as long as there's determination, desire, and willingness, the poor can do better. You have what it takes to do better in any situation. This power lives in you. Use the best tool at your disposal—yourself—to excel. Don't allow your shackles to tighten. Many have risen from the streets to become millionaires, and you can rise from the ashes and became inspirations.

Don't adjust to your conditions or embrace what others say is your destiny; make the sacrifices needed to better your life. You might bleed along the way, but you can gain your freedom. Free yourself from disheartening living conditions of the poverty of poverty. Forget that the poverty of poverty is an embarrassment to humankind and a shame to society worsened by human ignorance, greed, and stupidity. Focus on getting where you need to be, and then enjoy life and give a helping hand to those in the abyss. Others have done it. Do I have to say, "So can you"? No. You already know that.

11

Employment

It wouldn't do much good to curse money for becoming the dominant form of survival and happiness, nor does it pay to plot the destruction of humankind simply because employment is the main money generator and 1 percent of population holds 90 percent of world's cash and assets.

The rich are responsible for the insufficiency and unfair distribution of money, but chasing them with machetes for a fair share of the money would be foolish. On the other hand, to believe that being jobless is a life crisis will help you stay off the train of economic chaos whose first stop is hell. Thinking of ways to be employed should keep you awake at night until you have a job. And I am pretty sure it does.

Even thinking of ways to stay employed or fearing losing your job could keep you awake at night despite good trends in the employment numbers—if the numbers are true.

Anyone telling you that the world of employment is not as crazy as it seems is lying to you, is clueless, or is your worst enemy hiding malice behind fake smiles. Employment in recent times doesn't give us much room to breathe.

Balancing employment and life's demands is increasingly daunting. People who are employed continue to feel unemployed and very frustrated. Migration and immigration continue to soar because people can't find jobs where they lived. The middle class is pretty much lost in translation. Students finish their education but then face the stress of finding jobs. This tragedy is worldwide, but developing countries suffer the most. But giving up hope of finding a job is to jump from the frying pan into the fire. Do whatever it takes to land a job, hopefully a good one.

Full-time students working part-time jobs are getting financial support from their parents—at least room and board with laundry. The help you're getting is a wind at your back. You can also choose employment guided not by your heart but by convenience—good pay, job security, and no employment hassle and related expenses. That requires some serious reading between the lines and filling in the blanks, but it leads to success. On the other side of the river is a thirty-five-year-old hurt by and unhappy with his low-paying job who has to take action before he runs out of time and ends up even more unhappy.

Why would anyone wait until it's raining to look for a raincoat, an umbrella, and a safe place to shelter? Don't be an idiot. Get as much money as you possibly can from your current job while you search for a better and higher-paying one before it's too late. Maybe you like your current job; your company must be glad to have you, so keep up the good work and plan for future raises and stepping up the ladder. If your raises are based on performance, make sure you perform at your best without killing yourself. Companies pay you about 60 percent of your worth or they don't profit from you, so look for ways to work smarter, not harder. But always be looking for better opportunities; a higher salary is always nice but not if it means greater stress.

Tricks

Whether you have a job or are looking for one, keep in mind that a smart move is to work for one company until retirement. You could accumulate up to four weeks or more of vacation. The longer you stay on your job, the easier it becomes, and your chances of moving up the ladder increase. On the contrary, if you quit a job after years of loyalty, dedication, and hard work, you lose all of the above.

Sean's job at a warehouse involved lifting 50 pounds again and again on a daily basis—9,000 pounds a day. His performance was below average, and he wasn't getting any raises. One day, he realized his efforts weren't paying off, so he decided to demand respect and better pay. He showed his college certificate in basic computer science to his manager, who was pleased with that but encouraged him to get a better job somewhere else.

A few of his friends and coworkers had encouraged him to go back to school and finish his degree, but he just listened to his gut and kept demanding respect, an easier job, and better pay. When that didn't work, he started threatening the company with safety violations, racism, discrimination—you name it—but his company had no time for his cries, threats, and bullshit and wasn't about to promote him anywhere.

Five years later, he was still the laziest and lowest-paid employee. Fortunately for him, his company started pushing him out the door. That caught his attention. He found another job in his field of expertise; he's starting his career from scratch at age thirty-five. Late is better than never, but why late if early is better?

Staying at a workplace until retirement demands serious homework especially when you're middle aged or close to it. It's great to hang around with a company until it satisfies your employment goals. If you can't, quit before it's too late; make sure that your work, not you, is your reason for your leaving; it's always better to leave than to be escorted out.

Winning Big

The best employment is self-employment, but entrepreneurship with or without a partner is tricky and challenging. Even if your father gives you $1 million and his support, learn the tricks of the game before you sit at the table of self-employment. Learn as much as you can about business management, and have a right-hand helper next to you to help you navigate the rough, shark-infested waters.

In the US, about 90 percent of startups don't take off. Those that do usually fold in five years. And yet, when the numbers work, self-employment is the man. But all jobs can be unfulfilling and challenging for a variety of reasons some of which are completely out of our control including market volatility.

Whether you're working for someone or for yourself, no matter how important or powerful you are today, you could wake up tomorrow out of a job. The nature of your business could change, and technology can make what you do obsolete. Bubbles burst. Bad management can cause bankruptcy. Sexual harassment and claims of racism, discrimination, sexism, or misinterpretation of your words can put you out of a job or your work.

If you're an entrepreneur, all of the above and the strategies of the giants—Google, Apple, Microsoft, Amazon, Facebook, Walmart, Home Depot, Lowe's—could be a gun to your head. You need to avoid being shot.

There's no cussing out the guy who invented work or complaining that you're the slave of money; you still have to make a living, but that's easier now than it was before. If your job serves you worse than your parents' jobs served them, the fault is yours. You're living with less and are a member of the losers' club. If you're not grabbing everything in reach, you're being lazy and are living a sinful life.

There will be time when government will have total control of its people and life will be just fun and games. Our best friends will no longer be dogs; they'll be robots, cyborgs, and machinery run by artificial intelligence. Social security is from birth to death. Only big brains will help us live happily and without worries. I am not sure such living conditions would be the greatest, but who cares? Either way, this reality, although on a fast track, will get here only hundreds if not thousands of years from now. You and I can only envision it with jealousy and envy or sadness and sorrow for those who will have to live at that time. Therefore, worry not about it and wait not for it. By contrast, do what it takes to get the upper hand so you can live your dream life. Don't settle for low-hanging fruit when you're capable of climbing the tree for the best fruit.

Once you find your dream job, embrace it, but don't count on its being your dream job forever or you could be in for some nasty surprises. Unforeseen circumstances could cause you to lose your job no matter how hard you work. Also, never consider yourself an irreplaceable employee. The longer you've worked, the more you should prepare yourself for layoffs or being fired over minor issues especially if your job is low tech.

You might be a very loyal employee, but your company's loyalty will go only so far. If it gets to the point that you're no longer needed due to advances in technology for instance, you could be shown the door nicely or roughly. No company puts its employees' needs ahead of its needs. So if you're working, prepare yourself for unemployment. The irony or the beauty of this is that when you're prepared for a storm, it never comes.

Always make sure that your job will meet your needs and serve you well; only you fully understand what those needs and your capabilities are. Prepare yourself for your dream job, and if you have your dream job, prepare to advance in it. If you're unhappy there or unemployed, today is the day to change your direction.

12

Finances

IT FEELS THAT THE WORLD'S upside down and inside out or hell's on earth giving nightmares to all and leaving the elderly in distress, veterans homeless or fighting PTSD, and children dying of hunger and starvation… The minimum wages of a hundred years ago for example provided more than the current $15 minimum wage in some states.

Today, people are poorer, madder, more frustrated, and more ready to explode. The reasons for this tragedy are countless, but financial calamity is the main culprit. Unemployment, inflation, and the high cost of living can make it impossible for people to become financially secure.

Capitalism is constantly bombarding us with gadgets designed specifically for making us buyers for life; it's working for our financial detriment. The lack of money—more likely its insufficiency—is the King Kong in the room alongside many little, annoying monkeys squeezing in. We have to take the blame for our misery and fix it.

Guilty as Charged

We give in to our desires to buy things just because others have them or because we want to be the first on our block to have them. We're drawn to things that come in fancy packages, but then what do we do? We simply toss those packages aside. We buy expensive shoes when cheaper ones would be just fine. We demand what we don't need and probably can't afford. These are created needs, not real needs. Unless we can afford the cool, we shouldn't be a fool.

Our lifestyles—drugs, smoking, and alcohol—and our neglect of our affairs of the heart are bad for our finances too. The only way not to be broke is to print money in our basements, but that comes with its own problems as far as the FBI is concerned. And being mobbed up is not appealing. We can waste money on many things, and money itself loses its value due to inflation. Only careful money management can save us, and that's a concept we have to pass on to our children at an early age.

It's sad and unfair that governments wants us to waste money and die broke because that's how they thrive. Can you spell *taxes*?

Money Management

Money management requires knowledge and willingness. It looks simple, but it's actually complicated, and it takes time to become a good money manager. For that reason, many of us say, "Screw this," and spend irresponsibly.

If you're serious about building your finances, start with a winner's mindset: don't settle for anything but progress. From there, add all the condiments to the soup until it's to your taste. I say that because while money management basics are universal, the strategies aren't and shouldn't be. In making your financial plans, keep in mind that life never loses an opportunity to throw us under the bus and make us walk under the shadow of death. The wealthy can survive many financial setbacks, but unless you've saved enough, one bad financial disaster could ruin you. Build a strong financial foundation and fortify it because the future could end up asking you for a lot of your money.

Capitalism has brainwashed us into believing that living large is the way to go. Don't get me wrong; I'm all for living large, but for me, that means being happy, empowered, and excellent rather than being a financial show-off. Live within your means and stay there. This great financial principle is almost impossible to practice and master, but when you do, you'll live large in all its senses and happiness will never leave you. Live large the right way. Size matters not especially when it doesn't fit. Don't be a fool or let anybody fool you. This game is a serious game; even financial experts have a hard time winning at it. Money management is something we have to study seriously.

Our financial worlds can spin out of control if we neglect them rather than giving them the attention they deserve. That's a challenge, but it's better to sacrifice a bit now and live happily forever after. Put your brain to work, and make your money obey your orders. Life is becoming more hostile to your pockets and bank accounts. In the world of finance, there's no such thing as business as usual. The demands on our money can outpace our financial growth.

The 2018–19 government shutdown (December 22, 2018–January 25, 2019, thirty-five days), stressed out and enraged so many people who couldn't work or had to work without pay. Those with no financial safety nets—enough saved up to cover their basics for six months—suffered the most. Financial safety nets have become a necessity, so start or keep funding one starting today.

Dear youngsters, your personal growth is directly proportional to your level of education and financial skills. This principle is alive and well in black, white, brown, green, red, purple, yellow, and undecided social groups. Try to apply the rules governing corporations for your personal and financial growth; every little bit of knowledge counts. Decide to live within your means; that's the first step toward financial security.

Money has ruled the world for the longest time, and it will continue to do so. Consider your finances the oxygen you need to survive because it is. Get some supplemental supply and then breath with ease.

13

Relationships

As we begin to understand the dynamic of life and the sacrifices it requires, we realize that we can't escape stress and frustration, madness and disgust, sadness and disappointment. At times, we find ourselves frail and distressed, close to giving up, or cussing out life. We take all necessary precautions to stay safe, happy, healthy, and sane, but we wake up bruised by the unmerciful whips of life. We endure pain and discomfort and hope to heal quickly. After all, it's almost impossible to have only pleasant experiences day in and out.

Experience tells us that serious sacrifices are demanded and that we have to think ahead to stay ahead of the game. But God almighty, why are relationships—the essence of life—so complicated and almost impossible to get right? Beautiful, rich, and talented girls for example can end up struggling and suffering while learning the ropes of relationships. Middle-aged people's journeys are filled with drama, frustration, and disappointment. The elderly carry their chins on their chests while they quietly dress their wounds of regret, deception, and madness brought on by relationships. Everybody who's been in relationships bears scars in their hearts.

Soon after we taste a relationship's water, we begin to swim hard to stay afloat. Yes, sadly, we haven't found ways to dive into the pool of love and excitement without hitting bottom head-first. We're getting hurt more often in many other ways. We continue to be failures. Some of the blame goes to biology and many other factors out of our control, but most of it goes to us, the smart idiots as chimpanzees would say.

Success and happiness in relationships cost us blood, sweat, tears, commitment, and determination to go on regardless of obstacles. This bittersweet journey hasn't changed its character, but it's evolved and revolutionized while we've simply fallen behind. We can get lost on many surprising corners, twists, and turns of relationships. Even when we put human stupidity and ignorance aside, our relationships are full of mysteries we may never crack, but we can be successful at relationships if we start building our castles of love strong from first brick—dating.

Let's Date

Dating—the first step on this relationship journey—splits into two roads: dating for the sake of dating, and dating for a ring.

When you're single, you're free of lots of responsibilities, but your sexual needs can push you to find someone to party with regularly. This means you're pretty much ready to smack whoever comes your way with no strings attached, zero compromises, and see you later. Or you rely on prostitutes where such are allowed. It might be satisfying to fly like that, but there are consequences—STDs and unintended pregnancies for instance—that can make you feel that you've been gored by some angel's horns.

Dating without compromises has become less expensive as female pride, empowerment, and financial independence allow guys to not assume full responsibility for the bill of the night. Ironically, expectations are higher too, and greed could push you into going on many dates.

Girls, even if your finances are on firm ground or you don't care how much you spend to leave a remarkable first impression, don't spend a million to look like a million. A beautiful pair of high heels, a new pair of jeans, sexy underwear, stops at the beauty salon and your manicurist's, a beautiful necklace, earrings, and a handbag to close the deal can set you back $500 easily, so be smart: dress cheaply but nicely, look like a million dollars, and take the jackpot of the night home to bed if that's the plan. If at the end of the night, all you've gotten is disappointment, you won't be desperately pissed off. And keep in mind that dating without compromise is walking on a slippery road, so beware.

When you're dating for a ring, apply all your knowledge of relationships. Fortunately, you're surrounded by all you need.

Here are some dating heads-up for your consideration to stop nasty surprises from laughing at you. I bet you have or will experience the following examples no matter how tragic, absurd, or comic they sound.

Don't kiss your dog on the mouth to show your love for pets. Your date might have seen your dog eating feces, messing with rotten food out of a trash bin, or sniffing something disgusting. Don't involve your pets at all.

Don't leave your thick, twelve-inch vibrator in plain sight. Your date might refuse to party with you because he's found out about your wishes, needs, and desires. And clearly, he's not your match.

Keep photos of your past loves out of sight too.

Don't just spruce up your house; clean it thoroughly.

Make sure the bathroom is clean.

Whoever picks up an STD on a first sexual encounter is a dumb sucker. Worse if you get pregnant or impregnate someone.

If you have a condition, you should mention it before it reveals itself in an awkward situation.

Don't take a couple of M&Ms or any edible resembling a pill to prove you're on the pill and leave another dozen in the drawer. It's almost guaranteed that your date will peek around for verification. Don't steal a baby from a man; ask nicely for one. Tricks are the road to hell.

Don't use sex as a strategy to lose weight, relieve frustration, or exact revenge.

Don't borrow your friend's car for a date, and don't even think about using the hearse of the funeral home you work at to pick up your date.

Be considerate: if your date doesn't measure up or his performance sucks, tell him, not your friends or people online.

Let honesty take you there. And if you must lie, leave your grandmother out of it. Everybody knows that "My grandmother is in hospital" is a lie.

Dating can lead to exciting social and sexual experiences, and it could drop the relationship of your dreams right into your lap as long as you play your cards right, read between the lines, fill in the blanks, and stay ahead of the game.

By the way, if the father of your date has threatened you because you're a loser without aspirations, take that as a wake-up call and a motive for sweet revenge when you get your shit together and excel. And if you can run fast enough, tell him that his daughter doesn't have much to offer either.

Why Does It Go Bad?

What doesn't go bad? Reality walks toward bad and ultimately to complete destruction; it's as simple as that. It would be foolish to think relationships were an exception to this rule. It would be nice if they were, but unfortunately, relationships have many rotting agents with a straight arrow ready for deployment such as irreconcilable differences, financial strain, the meddling of the in-laws, religious beliefs, political affiliations, and the sniper on the roof—cheating.

Up close and personal, partying suffers a decline of frequency and quality. Yes, sex four times a week will reduce to one time a week, once a month ... The excuses increase, and when there's action—finally!—an ultimatum like, "Hurry up! I have things to do. My show starts in ten minutes"—so on and so forth. Your first name is no longer replaced by baby, darling, sugar, honey, or sweetheart. And your financial support becomes more important than your love and care. All of the above are some of the low cards on the table that result in a lack of appetite for intimacy, the greatest ingredient for a delicious relationship meal.

In the meantime, you can play your cards right and sail through rough waters without losing the enjoyment of the trip. It takes a little bit of work. Actually, it takes an incredible amount of work, but it's worth it, and you can do it.

Another way to enjoy the thrills of your relationship is to understand and cope with its reduction of amusement as it goes through the inevitable decline of aging, and always look for opportunities to be unpredictable. If your passion and lust are depleted, do something about it. You'll be happy in your relationship and not even notice that it had ever gone sour.

Could It Get Better or Worse with Time?

Age represents experience. Experience represents confidence. Confidence allows us to move on our journey with ease and a certainty of success. On that note, we have reasons to believe relationships get better with age—or they should. The problem is that relationships are very tricky and cannot stand on their own for long; they require daily maintenance. Unlike wine, which gets better as it ages, relationships can get worse with age, and the older the relationship, the greater the workload. If you're in for the sacrifice, your relationship can improve with time. But if you choose to let that river run its course, you can be sure of ending in an abyss with a flood of problems choking your relationship to death.

How many times do we need to hear that nothing is more crucial than communication in relationships? (Well, actions in the bed are, but there's no need to mention them.) Then comes the duty of each partner to assume his or her obligation to keep the relationship as smooth as it can be.

Cheating

We're born as innocent angels carrying genes of supremacy that drive us to victory at all costs. As we grow, we understand that this eagerness leads to a bad winning strategy—cheating. But we don't let go of it as we've realized that no matter what musical genre is dominant, everybody's playing in the same key. Oh yes, there's not a game we play that we don't cheat at or sit next to a cheater during. The sad part is that despite our efforts to keep our cheating discreet, we're often caught and have to face the consequences.

In relationships, shame and consequences don't come from a desire to be a winner. Rather, they come from a bite we've taken or are taking on forbidden desires we couldn't resist anymore. As part of what defines us or as the consequences of our fall to Satan's enticements, we can only be guilty as charged because cheating comes in so many forms and makes it impossible for us to stay loyal and faithful. We can cheat by act, thought, or omission. What a trap!

In my days, according to Catholicism, slow dancing was not a sin unless it prompted the dancers to have naughty thoughts. We aren't wired like that; slow dancing prompts erections and dirty thoughts. Some girls will dance with you only once if they don't feel your hard penis on their inner thighs and vulvae. Some of them give you discreet kisses on your neck or bring your body as close as possible to theirs as if to say, "Please excite me as much as you can. I'm yours." And the cavalier, dying to impress her with his dancing moves and giving her a taste of what he's carrying in his pants, makes sure he doesn't spoil her moment, which could make her night. It's impossible to be that up close and personal and not have wild sexual thoughts and intentions. Biology makes us guilty as charged.

Here's another one. We can't escape looking at our friends' attractive lovers and not wish they were ours. More often than not, when guys have good visuals, they stay on our minds as recipes for masturbation at least. Similar scenarios happens to girls.

So cheating is something we should embrace without reserve, but we can't because we have revenge genes just as we have cheating genes. Both are constantly looking at each other with disdain and saying, "Why don't you die?" That's why every time we found out we'd been cheated on, we got enraged and got ready to go to war. We didn't want to hear the reasons; we just wanted to get even, and right away.

In a relationship, cheating spells catastrophe. The irony is that people who accuse us of cheating are as guilty as charged.

Why the denial instead of a confession? The answer to this question is easy: because of the consequences! The consequences of denial are never as drastic as those of a confession. Cheating could be the only remedy to keep sexual activity alive, and a denial is a magic pill while a confession could mean losing all the benefits of a relationship. In general, to confess cheating is to offer your head for sacrifice.

No partner would want to get through that; all partners would rather take chances with secrecy.

Who knew? My friend John Doe Q, who bragged constantly about knowing women inside and out, laid eyes on one of the most beautiful women in town (not Mary John! She was my high school crush.) He had looks and money, which made it easy for him to attract women. One day, he woke up to face the fact that not every news on April Fool's Day was fake news. His girl was having a piece of bread on the side; he had thought women were incapable of escaping his radar beam until he found out that John Doe Y would park on the street, wait for him to leave, and go party with her. And there was a white John Doe, age twenty-one, a control freak who murdered his white wife upon the birth of a black baby. And the John Doe number goes up with cheating stories. Some are unfortunately tragic. (The examples above do not imply that women's infidelity is an innate phenomenon stronger than men's. In fact, men are worse than women when it comes to cheating.)

What's in it? We might need to go deeper for that. Not everything in our DNA is good for us; some things can get us in all kinds of trouble or even bring death to our beds unannounced. The killer instinct, rage, and madness among many other undesired human phenomena are troublesome. But the truth is, troublesome is not necessarily bad, and bad is not necessarily troublesome. The killer instinct for example is there for our survival; it saved our ancestors from predators' attacks. Cheating, the evil monster in us, is not all Satan. In fact, our cheating genes never sleep. They're always on an important mission we can understand only by reading between the lines and filling in the blanks. Relationships try to maintain emotional balance; yes, a bad thing for a great cause.

A relationship that causes excessive stress, frustration, and depression makes life a living hell rather than an oasis of satisfaction, love, care, and respect. Cheating is medicine that heals relationship wounds and restores happiness. Now, this forbidden, clandestine sexual adventure is more than a party by two or an extra piece of bread to the soul. It brings hormonal balance, a closure to emotional wounds, a sense of supremacy, and much more. This pretty much explains why cheating has a seat at relationship's table despite the fact that we don't handle it well especially when we're victimized by cheating, which proves how big of a hypocrite we are.

I once asked someone why I had been cheated on and got for an answer, "Sorry, but I needed it, and I couldn't resist it anymore. I never had an orgasm like that before. I felt so light." To guys, cheating is an adventure, a thrill that makes them feel superior to the one cheated on, which fuels our desire for cheating. Many times, it comes from sexual dissatisfaction such as not getting head, boredom in bed, poor quality or quantity of sex, and so on.

Cheaters are dancing around a very hot fire and do so at their own risk. They might escape the flames, and they might not. It's their responsibility to never get caught or to confess to it but also to be prepared to face the consequences.

What are the lines here? The lines start in you. If you want to cheat, nobody can stop you, but fill in the blanks; understand that you shouldn't give reasons for cheating or you'll just extend the wings of a raptor. Everyone's a cheater. Cheaters aren't the ones who cheated; rather, they're the ones who got caught. And those who cheated and told others about it are idiots.

Can I Be Loved?

Of course you can be loved! Once you find yourself in a relationship, you can be sure you're loved unless you're filthy rich; it's never clear when fame, cash, and other assets are involved in a relationship. But in either case, there are sacrifices required for love and passion to grow to the feeling-loved point.

We tend to go to extremes to show we have what it takes to be chosen first, but then we neglect our responsibilities. This makes matters worse since the nature of relationships changes somewhat after a few parties behind closed doors and drastically once the ring is on the finger and the cake is cut. In the days, weeks, months, and years after that, doubts about being loved could spring up. To avoid such disturbing feelings, you want to bring more heat to your relationship starting with appreciation and respect and ending with until death do us part. Once you live by this principle, you can be sure you're loved more every day. If not, don't be afraid to demand that you should be loved clearly and openly.

Can I Be Loved Forever and Ever?

Have no doubts about the possibility of being loved forever and ever, but don't sit there and watch it fall from the sky into your heart because it won't. To be loved forever and ever, hold onto the behaviors that made you feel loved, improve them, and add new ingredients to replace those that were lost.

We're creatures who lose beauty and ability as we age. It won't matter how much we want to be there for our partners' satisfaction and happiness; our physical and physiological decline will not grant our wishes. The most important ingredient to cook a delicious relationship meal is sex. You won't be able to provide it with a frail physical condition and poor health, so eat well, exercise, avoid drugs, smoking, and drinking, and be willing to go out of your way to spice up the action under the sheets. Don't even think about telling me, "Easier said than done"; everybody knows that. But doing whatever it takes to stay ahead of the game of relationships will assure that you'll be loved forever and ever.

Common Ground

All relationships go through similar realities in different ways: love, passion, care, caresses, jealousy, senseless arguments and then back to love, passion, cares, caresses, jealousy, and senseless arguments over and over. After a while, this behavior can become a relationship's normal. And most of the time, we let our partners get away with things for the sake of the relationship. I guess you shouldn't change a thing if your purpose is fulfilled.

A better approach would be to reason with different viewpoints, fight what's stupid and detrimental to the health of your relationship, and protect your relationship's defining bricks. It's your duty to find common ground in your relationships. Don't feel shy about swallowing pills you're sure that will do the trick, and try new ways of promoting joy and happiness. Some relationship rules and taboos are worth respecting because they're pretty much common denominators in relationships. But they will deliver better results in combination with the defined bricks of your relationship. Let's emphasize the *your*.

All Else Has Failed. What Now?

Since we're the product of unity and collaboration programmed to seek a relationship for the continuity of our species, being together is a reality we must obey and should respect. For the most part, we try our best to carry on. When one relationship doesn't work, we seek another, and another, and another. We learn from the relationships we walked away from and use the experience on the next ones. And yet, time and time again, we're whipped left and right, up and down, and are bruised, cut, and asking, "Why?"

Thankfully, our resilience gives us the strength to go on and our experience makes us wiser. But not all relationships are meant to survive. After hitting bottom head-first many times and having turned over every stone, it's time to call it quits.

Quitting here doesn't mean getting up and leaving; it means evaluating the situation and applying what you've learned. It means taking the time necessary to prepare for your departure in certainty that this is your last and living determined to find ways to ensure you're done with breakups. You know it well—Each time you call it quits, you shoot yourself in the foot, go to the back of line, and start over. An exit strategy could be your savior.

Exit Strategy

Most of us have found ourselves in dead-end relationships that were singing really bad songs. Yes, we slept on the couch or in our cars, called our friends for places to crash, and knocked on Mom's door. We stayed up all night long wondering. The translation for that was that we screwed up big-time and have to pay for the crime.

But the payback now is not for being an obnoxious jerk who didn't care about nurturing a relationship; it's for not having an exit strategy. Since the roads of divorcing, breaking up, and separating are long, let's cut to the chase and claim the prize—the exit strategy. The idea is great, but its implementation is tricky.

You see, whatever relationship we're in, until death do us part is in the back of our minds. It's normal in relationships and especially marriages for husbands and wives to work toward common goals and be two bodies with one soul; that makes sitting down with our partners to discuss an exit strategy very awkward. I'm sure our first question would be, "Why?" And from there, the conversation could go in circles as one partner tries to explain that there's no malicious intent in this game and that an exit strategy would strengthen the relationship instead of weakening it while the other partner just can't digest what's happening. Be cautious on your approach, and select your words very carefully especially for a relationship that's usually rocky; otherwise, an exit strategy could be forced.

But who has an exit strategy? Isn't that why we hang on for a little longer in a relationship that's not working or become devastated when we split up? Regardless of how much love, trust, and devotion a relationship rides on, an exit strategy should exist because it's a lifesaver. Don't be a fool. Once your feet are embedded in solid ground, you shouldn't fear windstorms, but it doesn't hurt to be prepared for them.

Those in relationships dominated by senseless arguments and foolish accusations should have an exit strategy. It requires no more than a separate account to cover moving expenses and rent after a split and an agreement on issues such as child support, custody, and other responsibilities. Yet the best strategy is to never have to use an exit strategy.

Is It a Miracle, Luck, or Something Else?

The answers are none of the above and all of the above. To let a relationship walk its walk is to cross a busy intersection blindfolded hoping not to get hit. This is a stupid move we do just about all the time, but we're surviving; sometimes, we put minimal effort into a relationship and sail through mildly rough waters that pose no threat. Other times, we give it all we've got but still face relationship nightmares. More often than we think, relationships that were not meant to be or were neglected stand up to all kinds of storms. For that reason, I believe miracles, luck, and something else play roles in the health and happiness of relationships, but here's what rocks and deserves a gold medal.

God must be listening, the universe must be in harmony, the stars must be aligned, and Earth must be spinning impeccably for our best wishes to come true by snapping fingers. Maybe once in a billion blue moons, this happens to creatures very far away, but not to us humans. Therefore, we can never rely on miracles and luck to make our dreams come true. We realize that taking matters into our own hands brings far better results. We also realized that a great partner is an outstanding substitute for miracles, luck, or that something else. In fact, a great partner makes them bow and go home.

Relationships might be beasts with seven heads, but they're crafted wonderfully from beginning to end for the enjoyment and thrill of two people who decided to unite, help one another reach goals, and share life, sex, and intimacy with one another forever. Partners help each other open doors to greater achievements as they combine forces. As the best stone with which to build your empire, a relationship is an extension of ourselves. We forget that relationships are like the wine in a chalice; they could've been ordinary but now they're sacred.

Whether you're incredibly good looking or not, don't accept whomever destiny finds for you right off the bat. Seek until you find your desire, and make your relationship a shining star. Whether you're black, white, yellow, green, or purple—rich, filthy rich, or destitute—illiterate or very smart—you can dig deep for ways to defeat the side effects of relationships. If the soulmate of your dreams turns out to be a slick who's sleeping with everybody in town or has become the scum of all scums who's sucked you dry and left you for nothing, you can still thrive. Pick up what's left, and rebuild yourself stronger.

If you're in a happy relationship, keep on doing what you've been doing and stay vigilant to intruders. When you find yourself on the other side of the river, pick up the broken pieces, breathe in and breathe out, walk to your inspirational spot, and find ways to make your relationship brand new.

If you're single, I hope you're seeking a relationship. After all, body heat feels nice in the cold temperatures of this crazy life. If you choose to stay single without sex, you're depriving yourself of happiness and a sense of belonging and stripping your body, mind, and spirit of the best nourishment. Find ways to dodge or cope with stress, frustration, and depression as the immediate consequences and the health complications that follow that.

Our relationships are among the most important steps on our journeys but are among the most dangerous—to our shame. When we mess up, it's like a beast with seven heads has slammed us down and left us for dead. The good news is that there are plenty of ways to avoid such tragedies.

Let's avoid bouncing from one relationship to another hoping to one day land softly and be settled for life. Youngsters, you get to be the exception, but your game shouldn't go on forever. The sooner you get on with the program the better. The program is to ask for help with your flight plan so you can steer around those who don't care about whom they go to bed with. Chances are that they don't know that he who sleeps with dogs wakes up with fleas. Accept advice especially from your family and friends, and then take off, follow your flight plan, and monitor your progress. Whenever you're off course, make corrections and proceed with confidence.

I am sure fully grown adults have crashed and burned more than once. You have to avoid one more incident; it could be deadly. Learn from your experiences and mistakes as well as others' tragedies. Wisdom and grit should help you find medicine that works for all illnesses in your relationship. And to the elderly, I say that from now on to the end, enjoy the ride with as much love, peace, and harmony whether or not the road is smooth, under clear skies, and with plenty of sunshine.

To worship a bird with body, mind, and soul ensures it'll never get away. Those who carry knowledge and wealth in forsaken hearts live sad, empty lives.

14

Drugs

IT DIDN'T TAKE US LONG to realize the great dangers in the jungle. If the beasts looking at us as delicious meals didn't make us run for our lives, the bushes were poking us and giving us scrapes and cuts and insects were biting us for meals, fun, and revenge. Ripe but poisonous fruit tempted us. There weren't pharmacies, nurses, or doctors. But as the chosen ones endowed with the ability to observe, analyze, experiment, and solve problems, we were watching what happened to our friends, enemies, and other animals. We ate the fruits they ate and avoided whatever killed them. We cared for each other. We were determined to survive.

We used leaves for protection against infection when we got cut. Curiosity made us drink tea and discover that it was medicine. Our curiosity grew and gave us science.

The technology got better, and medicine improved drastically.

We were vaccinated as children to avoid horrible illnesses. Then we grew to rely on drugs to help us feel better and cure and even eradicate illnesses. The elderly depend on many drugs for different ailments. We simply cannot live without drugs despite their side effects.

Thanks to the devil, who never sleeps whenever there's the smell of money in the air, here we are in a drug pandemic. Young and powerful lives have been lost, and families have been shattered. The fight seems endless and the chance of victory seems slim in part because the battlefield of drugs is expansive and complex.

Addicts, their families, and the government struggle to find solutions to drug abuse and its consequences. This fight is ugly, costly, and heartbreaking. Drugs prescribed by doctors have given us problems—side effects—because, well, all drugs have side effects, some minor and others significant, but they're a million miles away from those of illegal drugs, prescribed pain killers, and mismanaged prescriptions that can lead to addiction.

We spend tons fighting illegal drugs. The Addiction Research Center, part of the US Public Health Center, got its start in 1935 in Lexington, Kentucky. Pretty much every year since, the government created and modified acts related to drug use, addiction, and trafficking. And yet, on October 26, 2017, the president of the US declared an opioid crisis that was killing almost a hundred people a day—a national health crisis. What a shame on governments still far behind in this game! The power to solve drug problems lies in us.

Taking the Bull by the Horns

Patients. If you've been prescribed drugs, whether you're young or old, take them as prescribed; do not become addicted to them. Your doctor has taken this into consideration, but your self-awareness is as important as your doctor's monitoring of your health. Keep your prescription out of reach of other people, especially children and teens.

Addicts. Addicts, you're on the most dangerous part of the drug battlefield. The shadows of death have nailed you to the cross. You're a sacrifice to the devil; there's not enough money to cover your needs. Your chances of survival lessen every hour. Your integrity and respect are in a nosedive. Your days are numbered unless you free your minds.

It doesn't matter how messed up or deeply dependent on drugs you are; you can still clean yourself up and become inspirations to others. That journey could be torturous but not as much as your hopeless daily lives are, and there's a reward waiting for you at the finish line. The devil might have stolen your means of excellence, but he can't eradicate the strength in your soul. Take a deep breath, reach out, and shine like the stars you are.

Dealers. Sometimes, life handles us a bunch of low cards, and nothing but desperate measures can pull us out of the abyss. If that's your situation, leave the table before tragedy strikes. If you're at a drug-dealing table and making a name for yourself, if your empire is growing and your dreams are coming true, now's the time to reroute your journey. Dealing drugs is a dead-end venture with beasts and monsters along the way.

Seek alternatives to what you are doing as hard as that will be. Sure, with weed and other drugs being lifesavers, people selling such drugs are actually doing good for some and making those of us preaching a drug-free life very unpopular. We want others to avoid what starts sweet and wonderful but ends up painful and deadly.

On the other hand, by appealing to drug dealers to pack their bags, we're creating nightmares for addicts who can't support their additions legally. The world is badly cursed by weed. Not everyone can get a medical card for it, and weed sold at dispensaries is very expensive. So dealers serve a purpose.

Solving problems created by illegal drugs is a huge challenge for people and governments. After we read between the lines and fill in the blanks, we'll conclude that drug dealers do more harm than good.

Uncounted for. We, the lucky ones who are not addicted, must keep our guard up and our reflexes sharp. The devil has his eyes on us, and one small slip or stumble and we're caught in his net

Parents. Parenting has become a long trip to hell already, and then come drugs like a chameleon to whisk our children away. Our first responsibility is to ensure we're keeping our teenagers and children safe from drugs. Marijuana, now legalized in many states even though it's federally illegal, is considered by health organizations to be a drug. Whether or not marijuana is a drug in your mind, smoking it with your teenagers is like approaching the gates of hell and dragging them along. Its popularity makes it seems harmless and not addictive, but don't believe that; it's detrimental to your health and finances.

Many addictions are side effects of the medicines we take. It's a shame that we allow drugs vital for safeguarding our health to become actually detrimental to our health. Regardless of how we got into this mess, we can manage it and avoid future tragedies. Because the government can't get this beast under control, it's up to us to do that. Let's begin by internalizing that drugs can throw us off the throne of heroes and down to the basement of stressed-out and depressed losers. Let us protect ourselves from drug dependence.

Don't be shy about your misfortune. The more people know about your condition, the greater the chances are that you can get help. You were born a winner, but you have to exercise your power to keep on being a winner. Even when a fall from grace makes you look disgraced, you can repair the damage. If some can dig tunnels and escape maximum security prisons, you can escape your addiction. Rehabilitation is possible even if you tried it in the past but did not succeed. Don't be discouraged because you've tried many times in vain; keep trying until your wounds are nothing but faded scars. You're not looking for one more failed attempt; you're after one successful result.

Destiny is a jerk. More often than not, destiny played a little too rough with us and we woke up in a snake pit with many bites, but we didn't sit there with arms crossed hoping to die. We got out and sought help. Even if our current misfortunes are our fault, resilience is part of our genetic makeup. We can reach out to its power for dignity, integrity, and worth.

Stop giving your body what it wants and give it what it needs. That means not increasing your drug usage. Fight to reduce how much you swallow, smoke, or inject. I'm not a drug user, but I have friends who are addicts, and I have witnessed their struggles and suffering when they've tried to quit. Some things get worse before they get better, but living a drug-free life can be the reward.

Listen to your positive voices. Your family and friends are there for you. Take the help they can give you.

Think outside of the box. Surrounded by your kind, you feel no urge to look for an exit; everyone you see is an addict. Drugs can keep you in the land of losers. We're the only creatures with the power to think of something and act on it; cash in on that and clean yourself of any mud on you especially mud with the power to keep you broke, miserable, and ashamed all the way to the grave.

Let's honor Nancy Reagan's slogan—"Just say no to drugs." Honoring that appeal can save you from being another unfortunate young mind who ends up stoned to death. Whether you're drug free or an addict, fight drugs for your excellence and celebration of life. Do it for your honor despite that mean math teacher who told you that you wouldn't ever succeed. Do it for the people who cursed you because they supported you through taxes they pay. Do it for that heartless girlfriend or boyfriend who forsook you when you needed her or him the most. Do it for your family who abandoned you because they thought of you as a loser. Embark on a sweet journey of revenge, and prove that ordinary individuals can achieve the extraordinary.

15

Nutrition, Health, and Fitness

BAD THINGS COME IN THREES, but not every trio is malicious, and that includes nutrition, health, and fitness, the most productive trio. Every time we prioritize one of them over the others, we lose.

Nutrition

The nutrition we need for our survival is killing us. Obesity is result of too much food whether good or bad. We're victims of our success and idiots who dump food in the trash while children go to bed hungry if not die of starvation. Let's understand nutrition, health, and fitness so we can do better for ourselves and others.

The struggle for nutrition for growing populations has always been one of the King Kongs in the room. It made sense about 10,000 years ago to domesticate plants and animals, but as the population increased, so did the struggle to provide for it. And human stupidity poured salt into the wounds. Wars caused stunning losses of lives and agriculture land. People and governments struggled to rebuild from the rubble under social, economic, and health crises.

The Great Depression—a direct consequence of World War I, which ended in 1917—brought the world to its knees. And World War II rationed pretty much everything and nutrition first. After that war, people were fed up; the desire to live large sparkled a revolution and especially in the food industry. There was a need to feed people, replace those who had died during the war, and rebuild armies—as stupid as that last one sounds.

Nations were secretly fighting to emerge as number one after the war. After all, nutrition and economic power are the first two indicators of a nation's prosperity. Food had to be cheap so people's money could go far. And people were hungry for work, so road, railroad, highway, and housing construction stepped on the gas. People needed lots of energy, which food and beverages provided. Geniuses provided that in the form of junk foods, candy bars, and sugary drinks.

Back in my home, sugarcane, bananas, coffee beans, coconuts, peaches, mangoes, and oranges were gifts from the land; rural areas were paradises. It inspired me to be a good farmer, raise my family, and plan to die well nourished and happy. Then in the late seventies, the picture changed. Frequent droughts affected our paradise; crops were poor and very unpredictable. The decline was a worldwide phenomenon as was the struggle to put food on the table. So the geniuses revolutionized agriculture with pesticides, fertilizers and so on but with bad side effects that increased complications and other issues for humans caused by what they ate and drank. How counterproductive!

Health

My father seemed jealous of his friend who at age ninety said, "I don't know the doors of hospitals and pharmacies." I know the man my dad was talking about, but I don't remember his having been sick. I convinced my father that his friend could've been avoiding sick people, or relying on home remedies, or being among the very lucky.

Fortunately for us, later generations, science, and technology enabled big brains to come up with remedies for illnesses and diseases and surgical procedures that were successful. We're still victims of cancer, the flu, the coronavirus, and other diseases and viruses, but we've done all right.

Gimmicks. Health insurance, doctors, and hospitals seem to be in a cat-and-mouse chase. Health insurance companies try to pay less to doctors, who perform unnecessary surgeries to make up for that. Hospitals have to pay medical staffs, run their facilities, and provide good health care in the face of competition, and all three entities must milk every penny out of patients they can all because health care is a business.

Doctors and hospitals have to run their practices as businesses, but there is a thin line separating integrity and greed. Some doctors crossed it by prescribing painkillers that resulted in the opioid crisis.

Liability. The US is a large tree rooted in law and order. Everyone involved in taking care of patients must be sure of what they're doing or trouble will knock on their doors. Doctors can lose their licenses and can be sued. As much as they want to save you a buck or two, they must play by the books to avoid nightmares. To play it safe, they recommend a test and visits to specialists. In fact, if there was a diagnostic test a doctor recommended but that a patient refused to have done, you can bet that that will be documented in that patient's files for the doctor's protection.

People's demands. We Americans demand excellent care from customer service up to medication. The building itself must be nice outside and impressive inside with coffee shops, lobbies with beauty pageant contestants behind desks, top staff, and state-of-the-art equipment. And food there must be delicious or we'll never go back. This demand for high quality increases the costs of the services hospitals provide. And then we want a prescription that will make us feel better overnight and 100 percent fine in three days. Popular medication will not bring this kind of fast relief. What we demand is expensive. Insurance might refuse to pay full price, and our pockets will cry.

Culture of drugs. We've become addicted to medications. We take them to stay awake, go to sleep, for a minor headache, cold, fever, pain, discomfort, stress, frustration, depression, anxiety, and hallucinations. And then we take medications to counter the side effects of the medications we're taking—the dog is chasing its tail.

The problems of health care are bigger than providers and governments are. Until we read between the lines and fill in the blanks to stay ahead of the game, such problems will only grow as will our anger and frustration and our dependence on drugs.

Fitness

There isn't a lot of mystery with fitness because we have total control over it. We can join a fitness club or have home gyms. We can jog, swim, and bike. There's no rock to throw at fitness. Alleluia! With that said, let's look at the three fundamental factors of a good life: nutrition, health, and fitness. But first, let's learn with the masters.

Brain. When we cut ourselves in the kitchen, we feel pain right away. The brain forces us to feel it because its responsibility is to keep us alive and well. If we get in a bad car accident, the brain puts us to sleep right away or we see everything happening in slow motion. All our motors skills are denied any request because the brain doesn't want to do anything right then except save us. So there's no adrenaline rush and no panicky feelings that put excessive demands on our hearts. When we're in a coma, our brains are upset because they have not brought us back to life promptly. And if we die, our brains die of self-disappointment.

If we neglect that cut we got in the kitchen, it could become infected, and we could even lose it. The brain could only shrug at that; it did its best to tell us, "Hey stupid! Fix that cut or else!"

Biology. No child likes to take medicine. This is because our bodies work hard to keep us healthy and don't want any help unless it's an extreme situation. Our bodies fight infections, viruses, and bacteria. They're happy to do so; it's their duty. If we take medication for a sickness right away, we're increasing the fight for our cells since almost all medications come with side effects. This is not to say we should stay away from medications, but we should take them only when necessary.

While we're born to hate medication, we're always ready to play, and that means we have to be nourished, healthy, and fit. Let's not give our brains a chance to call us idiots who killed themselves with bad diet and lack of exercise.

Nutrition, health, and fitness are the inseparable triplets we needed for our activities in the caves and out in the wild. Then we took Tarzan's looks, strength, and endurance as inspiration and created fitness clubs and home gyms. We realized that when nutrition, health, and fitness joined forces, we could move mountains. If taking care of our nutrition, health, and fitness is complicated and discouraging, too bad; we have to face the music or die pissed off. Since we don't want that, here are some ways we can become nourished, healthy, and fit.

- You are what you eat. Watch the quality and quantity of what you take in.
- "There's an insufficiency of healthy food for 7 billion people" is a false statement. We trash food to keep prices high.
- "There's an insufficiency of organic food for 7 billion people" is a true statement. We invented pesticides and fertilizers out of necessity to increase the supply of food. Even if there were enough organic foods,

they'd cost too much for many people. Inorganic is not necessarily unhealthy.

- "Financial handicaps are the gorilla in the room" is a fair but not an absolute statement. The majority knows how to eat well but can't afford good food. If you empower your finances, your health, nutrition, and fitness will follow. On the other side of the river, some people have all money in the world and still eat badly.
- Save a penny or two by making your food stretch. Dilute a bottle of any concentrated juice and you won't need another bottle tomorrow, and you will have cut the sugar content in half.
- Few can eat lots of foods that are bad for them without severe consequences. Even if you're one of the lucky ones, eat bad stuff in moderation.
- You might need to start cooking your own meals more often and including lots of fibers, greens, and fruits. Our taste buds are dumb and easily fall for what is sweet, looks yummy, and tastes delicious. More often than not, these kinds of foods leave us with obesity, diabetes, high cholesterol, and high blood pressure to deal with.
- Follow your doctor's instructions. So many patients don't finish their course of medication and end up sick again because some cousins of the bug they got never died.
- Don't be so eager to swallow a pill or drink a medicine. Get together with your body and define what your best home remedies are. They're cheaper and usually without side effects.

- We left the caves of Africa and populated the world because we were always looking for the next better thing beyond the horizon. Up close and personal, after spending eighteen months—or even less—in bed, you'll have to relearn to walk. And if you stay inactive in your later years, your mobility will be hindered and your days could be numbered. Stay as active as you were meant to be.
- "Everyone's busy" is true, but "No one has time for physical exercise" is bullshit. And so is "I'm too tired to exercise." You can exercise while you're cooking or watching YouTube. You're never too tired for some aerobics or floor exercises. Same for sex.
- "If there's a will, there's a way." Many little and big menaces obstruct our path to success in nutrition, health, and fitness. Drugs, alcohol, and cigarettes for example are big menaces that alone have enough power to take us down. When they combine forces, we can become unable to get and hold a job, and chances are that we'll always be too messed up to eat right and exercise.

Nutrition, health, and fitness are weird triplets; one takes a punch and the others feel the pain. We can't live happily unless they're under control and balanced; then they become our allies, our tools. Ancient people ate organic foods, breathed pure air, and died at age thirty-six. Currently, we eat junk and breathe polluted air but can live to a hundred if we play our cards right. Therefore, stop eating all that's available and then suffering the consequences. As the games continue to be increasingly more complex, you must read between the lines and fill in the blanks to be the leader you are instead of the follower you chose to be.

Let's all live healthy lifestyles supported by exercises and a balanced diet. The reward is a long, happy life at an affordable price.

16

How Short Is a Hundred Years?

A HUNDRED YEARS SOUNDS LIKE an infinity, but people can live that long. During childhood up to young adulthood, the idea of a hundred years wraps around the world ten times, but to a forty-eight-year-old who's been living in his mom's basement for seven years and just decided to get his GED, find someone to marry, and raise a family under the roof of their own, a hundred years is nothing more than a couple of laps around block. Since our lives aren't limited to those two examples, let's dig more into what makes some lives longer and others shorter.

Untouchable Time

We waste our first dozen or so years just learning the ropes. Then we enter puberty and dance with adolescence for another seven to ten years. During these two phases, we generally take life as it comes. We enjoy time as if it were standing still. Fun is fun, and we don't have many responsibilities.

At age twenty-one, we start taking some bulls by the horns. We're confident adults with dreams and are making progress toward fulfilling them, but then things can slow us down and disappoint us. We become lazy or start engaging in activities that don't propel us forward such as drinking or doing drugs, or we start stumbling over obstacles such as these.

Government. The success or failure of citizens depends on the management of a country. If it's rich, democratic, and run well, people can live happily. A poor country with oppression as a political system dominated by corruption leaves people facing headwinds.

Time. Not every year or decade is prosperous, and natural disasters, wars, terrorism, and crime can slow economies down and make survival tough, while an economic boom allows people to cruise. A free ride!

Finances. We always need money, and as we get older, we need more of it. If we don't develop and stick to a budget, trouble's living on our doorsteps. We could lose many nights of sleep worrying about our debts and past-due bills.

National resources. In poor countries, the chance of earning a decent living is low, and that can shorten some people's journeys; some will die at age forty-five due to the lack or the cost of medical care.

Relationships

It takes two to tango. No species needs one another more than humans do. No species can accomplish more than humans can. No species worships relationships more than humans do. Marriage is simply the ultimate milestone on the list of our achievements. If we let it ride on a roller-coaster and stop at a lawyer's office to sign divorce papers, "It takes two to tango" will sound more like "It takes two to burn in hell." Divorces are big speed bumps that can stall our journeys to a hundred years. The more turbulent our relationships are and the longer they stay that way, the shorter will be the years we can enjoy.

Nutrition, Health, and Fitness

It actually takes three to tango; two dancers and a song. And so to have nutrition, health, and fitness in good shape is to tango all night long. The mood is great. The dancing floor is sharp. The songs are uplifting and motivational. The night will seem forever young, and when it comes to an end, it will be a blessed end. Having nutrition, health, and fitness working in harmony is like being well prepared for a marathon. It means not having to go to the hospital or a doctor's office; it's a strong tail wind on our journey to a hundred years.

Genetics

Nothing plays a bigger role on the journey of life than our genetics. They determine whether we'll be tall, healthy, strong, intelligent, and long lived or not. Some of us respect our heritages and genes and live wisely. They make every day count and don't let any opportunity go to waste. They squeeze as many gracious moments as possible into their daily activities while staying focused on improving themselves. Others, not so much, and they end up living uninteresting and short lives.

A friend of mine told his twenty-five-year-old son, "Hurry up and have a baby. I wanna be a grandfather before I die." Eighteen months later, he became a grandfather—another milestone. He wants to stay ahead of the game and make his hundred years last more than that and enjoy them fully.

My brother and many friends became diabetics and were cursed by other health complications due to drinking, bad behavior, and neglect. I got bad news from my sister; her thirty-five-year-old neighbor had drunk himself to death and left his eighty-year-old mom all alone. I also heard of someone who adventured in love and lust without boundaries or concerns about STDs and died at age forty-two of AIDS. Tons of phenomena out of our control can shrink our longevity, but it's a shame when we're victims of self-inflicted and premature death. Our genes might've given us long lives, but our stupidity can shorten them.

Humans

My niece was nineteen when she had her first child who was born unresponsive; his hundred-year journey didn't even make it to the starting line. In February 2018, a mother in Brockton, Massachusetts, killed her two sons by stabbing them up to fifty times. War, organized crime, terrorism, mass murders, politics, hatred, bias, ignorance, greed, and so on have cut many lives short. Others die of medical errors and mistakes, neglect, violence, and stupidity.

We should kiss the feet of nurses, doctors, soldiers, and all others who put their lives at risk daily so we can live free and pursue happiness. They're extending our hundred years at the expenses of their own.

Happiness and Purpose

When the Athenian government ordered Socrates, the philosopher, to stop his teachings and live or drink hemlock and die, he chose the potion and took his philosophy with him to the grave. Rumor says he declared his gladness to philosophize with his dead peers.

Bob Marley died at age thirty-six of skin cancer found under a toenail. He turned down his doctor's advice to have the toe removed to save his life and chose to sing and perform instead. He died very young but happy. I am sure there are many more similar examples.

Since it matters how long you live but not as much as how happily you live, define your happy life and fight to live it. Don't be among those who dream of getting their own houses, marrying, and starting families but do nothing to achieve their dream. They'll die without going on even one vacation overseas.

Stick to your dreams, pay attention to what's important on your journey, and be cautious of what can make your journey a nightmare. If you've lived happily and achieved your dreams, your life span is long regardless of how long you've lived. The opposite is a shame. And there you have it. A few examples of different contributing factors into extending or shrinking human life span—now about a hundred years.

Life's not short because we say it is; life's short period. Our first heartbeat—not our first birthday—is the start of our hundred-year journey. At whatever age you become aware of the millions of things that can cut your journey short, prepare to handle the bumps on your road. Don't allow procrastination, laziness, or pessimistic voices to shorten your journey. Don't wait until you're retired to curse life; start cursing it when you're eighteen and even more when you're thirty. Then pack as much empowerment as you can fit into your hundred-year backpack. Live and live some more all the way to the end. At seventy, don't say, "I'm just waiting to die"; say, "I'm still kicking!"

Be aware of everything that threatens your longevity and everything that enhances it. Fight to minimize the impact of the former and maximize the impact of the latter. You've heard of people who were given six months to live, refused to accept that death sentence, changed their behavior, fought their diseases, and lived for decades past that. On the other hand, drugs, alcohol, and cigarettes have snatched the lives of thousands and continue to do so—such a shame. Don't call your game over too quickly; prepare to run a marathon.

We humans are the true mystery of all mysteries. To our astonishment, the deeper we dig, the more mystery we discover. Nothing says we can't honor our honor as the rest do. We can embark on the journey of extending our lives.

By the way, we die three times: when we're dead, when we're buried, and when all who know us are no more. You can extend your hundred years, and it'll be worth it.

17

The Science and Technology Revolution

We humans are truly the chosen ones; we can think of ways to create the means to deal with life instead of hiding in our caves. We can come up with ways to get beyond where we were yesterday and make our lives easier and more exciting, prosperous, and fulfilling.

Anthropology says that it all started 14 billion years ago with the big bang; about 4 billion years ago, the first simple cell arrived. And then, evolution got up and began the march to multicellular creatures about a billion years ago. Living things diversified and ultimately resulted in species and subspecies that still carried the characteristics of that first single cell.

Mutations resulted in primates about 50 million years ago. But the best was yet to come, and it did about 2 million years ago—the arrival of humans. Humans' DNA is only 4 percent different from that of chimpanzees, but that 4 percent is significant; the chimps' time of domination was over. They stayed put while humans moved on.

That 4 percent difference allowed humans to plan, create, invent, implement, and thrive. Humans embraced their call of duty with passion, dedication, and determination. When they fell, they rested a bit and got back up. The other creatures envied them, but humans just shrugged that off.

About 400,000 years ago, *Homo sapiens* took the stage. They were the lucky bastards who had the master key for humans' journey of excellence, which was speeding up with the help of the wheel, and then trains, cars, planes, and spaceships. That's how we got here so fast. Who are the masterminds and drivers? The geniuses and technology companies.

The Boys Have Arrived

The big, tall guys are in town to rule. Their mission seems to be to gain the deepest understanding of our needs, wants, and desires so they can cover all our bases and then penetrate our minds to take us to destinations they've already selected as well as to places they're not sure about yet. They're smiling brightly, but they mean business. As the conductors on the train of the technology revolution, they're seducing us with sweets and candy bars. They're not worried about smart kids who are reluctant to ride their train. "Sooner or later, they'll come on board, too, and end up enjoying the ride," they say.

Oh yes, Apple, Google, Microsoft, Facebook, and Amazon control our lives. The future will be whatever they want it to be. So far, they've been enlightening and exciting us. They recognized, though, a need to do more than that to keep us hypnotized. For that, they've been busy not only on their quest but also competing and or cooperating with their father—the military. Military technology is twenty to thirty years ahead of that of the big boys. They have under their sleeves lots of astonishing stuff both great and devilish. I don't know if we should worry more about boys in town or their fathers or not worry at all. But it's a sure thing that the railroads of the science and technology revolution have some scary curves ahead some of which the big boys intentionally created while others are the side effects of their actions. Oh, I almost forgot ... Government's not our savior; we are.

Once you're with gloves on in the ring, you need to use your strategy against your opponent but also find ways to use his strategy against him. We have become properties of tech companies, but that doesn't mean we no longer have freedom and liberty; it's the opposite. Tech companies have given us more freedom and liberty, which we've been enjoying. As this game continues, we have to use technology to empower ourselves and make sure we don't end up as total losers. The boys in town are smart, but we're not so bad ourselves. We can put our skills and talent to work for our benefit.

Scary Curves

It all started with population increases. The instruments we were manufacturing by hand were unable to meet the demand for them, so we created machines to help us increase quantity. Machines became man's second-best friend. (And I don't think dogs minded that at all. If they did, what could they do about it?)

When we gave machines their own best friends—computers—that's when we took a bite bigger than we could chew. We invented machines and computers to help us, but the next morning, we woke up with robots, supercomputers, and artificial intelligence (cyborgs are in the basement awaiting fine tuning) that help us domesticate earth and conquer universes.

We humans aren't sons and daughters of some dumb animals; we're the chosen ones. Even if aliens leave us alone because we're no more than insignificant insects deserving no attention of their superior minds, we'll always be the chosen ones of planet Earth. Our intellects allow us to discover new and different things and make competition the name of the game. This approach is taking us too far ahead of the game and onto troublesome roads at an incredible speed. The minds behind designer babies and gene editing are worrying us about humans playing gods or beating evolution. We don't have certainty that what science and technology have under their sleeves won't break us beyond repair especially as we're designing robots empowered to make their own decisions and self-improve their intelligence.

The ugly picture is to wake up with superhumans carrying modified human DNA at war with robots we forgot to teach to respect their creators or having to fight for liberation from all the angels we created that have turned themselves into monsters with hidden horns. The creations of our imagination seem to be taking us to a mountain and letting us know that similarly to the speech we gave chimpanzees, strange creatures will let us know that our rule is over. That would be a tragic end of an adventure. How likely is this dystopian view of the end of the human species to happen? Let's find out.

Bad guys took a free ride on the train of human excellence. When good guys pushed them off, they somehow hopped back on. The stone and metal tools we invented to better our lives became weapons. The firearms we invented to expand our hunting venues and increase our safety in the jungle became weapons we used to kill each other on a massive scale. Grenades had to give way to bombs, so we don't kill just people but also destroy all means of survival for the survivors. The machines we created to take us from point A to point B quicker and safer became tanks, submarines, and jets. Always looking for ways to improve matters, we created atomic weapons.

We can't stop because the genes telling us to break and then fix things will never leave our blood. The creators taught us how to fish and left us at sea with fishing tools we needed. There's no doubt we've been fishing in what seems to be prohibited waters that might make us extinct. Despite all, our destiny is to fish for as long as there are fish. There's no such a thing as impossible no matter how draconian or dystopian. May the Almighty have mercy on us!

What Is It to You? And Why Should You Care?

To know that science and technology have taken over our lives and that we're not equipped to defeat them is to understand the consequences of this tragedy and map a way out of it using science's and technology's successes as models. We're winners at birth. We turned enemies into friends and used obstacles as triggers for finding solution for problems. Determination became an indispensable tool for our staying afloat. It's our duty to ensure that nothing takes charge of our destiny let alone turns us into slaves. Geniuses never felt satisfied with what they achieved regardless of how awesome it was. They honored eagerness to conquer the next great thing. Take that as inspiration for your excellence.

Say you're an honor student, a distinguished professor, an MVP, the best friend ever, an angel of a sibling, the best spouse, a healthy, wealthy, and wise person with zero regrets. You're an expert in life and clearly ahead of the game … You can still do better by incorporating the philosophical principles of science and technology and utilizing your tenacity to become a better you. Always work to improve yourself and your way of life. Don't resist curiosity begging you for action toward excellence. When you embark on a mission to excellence, each day is a reason for a celebration.

Science and technology should be cared for and used by all with a clear understanding of the benefits we can embrace and the bad consequences we should avoid. Science and technology have put us on path to paradise. Let's honor their sacrifices by soaring through life on the wings they've given us, on the air they've put beneath those wings, and the inspiration they've given us to fly.

Of course, we should be concerned about the speed of the science and technology train so we don't get blown away, but we shouldn't freeze. Besides, this train has no final destination; we do. No matter how incredibly intelligent machines might become, they'll always be the humans' creation. We're parents who do not allow our children to kick our asses. It'll take millennia for my thoughts to be proven right or wrong, so don't worry so much that you leave no room for happiness. Stay in control of what you can with the assistance of science and technology. Read between the lines, fill in the blanks, stay ahead of the game, and then fear no evil.

I saw two sparrows zigzagging in the sky maneuvering up and down in loops and crazy dives. One was responding to every single maneuver of the other and was only a couple of inches from it, but it couldn't close the gap. I was astonished by the speed, maneuverability, and accuracy of that chase. I thought, *Look at those tiny brains at work!*

And then I thought, *We humans, are the big brains!*

18

Can't Live. Too Busy Trying To

EVERYTHING BEGINS WITH MYSTERY, BEAUTY, and promise and evolves to even greater mystery, beauty, and promise. That prompts us when we're young to want to grow up and start enjoying it all. We believe that there's somewhere to be free of the torments of our elder brothers and sisters, the persecution of English and math teachers, and ignorant people. And more important, we can't wait to be free of our parents' constraints. "Freedom, please hurry!" we might shout. Well, we'd better be careful about what we wish for.

Before we know it, we're no longer mom's little angels and daddy's little princesses. We've just won the adolescence battle in which life tried to kill us and everybody looked for an opportunity to make us evaporate. We've finally crossed the special border to adulthood. Tired, dazed, and confused and hoping that the paradises in our heads are still there, we realized adulthood has arrived pretty much unannounced and faster than we'd hoped for and not quite as nice as we had anticipated.

Another ten years went by, and we felt that life had unleashed its vicious dogs on us. We were cursing life, cussing people out, and hating ourselves because we were trying our best to live but couldn't because we were too busy trying. What a shame. What happened?

It seems that suddenly, life changed from being a loving mother into a scary, creepy neighbor. Life, however, can be absolutely innocent in the chaotic struggles we face daily; the greater blame for them falls on us. First, let's meet a couple of culprits—loose cannons and utter evil—before we talk about our crimes.

Loose cannon. Wars, natural disasters, government's lies and false promises, national and international politics, population growth, terrorism, immigration, racism, discrimination, segregation, sicknesses and diseases, and much more are the vicious dogs biting us and leaving us frustrated and feeling deceived.

For example, right when we thought we could hope for global peace and thus global prosperity, Russia pretty much told the world, "You're so damn stupid and very wrong if you think the Soviet Union is no more." North Korea tested another long-range missile and pretty much told the world, "Kiss my ass if you don't like it. And beware, the US!" The US responded by pretty much saying, "Try me, Korea!" when the US warned China to play by the rules of the World Trade Organization or face the consequences. Then a US president ignored his campaign promises and started serving his supporters rather than everyone. We worry about losing our jobs to robots, automation, and immigrants. We're now afraid of shopping in malls or attending large gatherings due to the possibility of becoming victims of lunatics. Loose cannon are tampering with our lives.

Utter evil. Personal things we should have total control of such as our health, nutrition, fitness, relationships, and so on are dominated by hundreds of factors out of our control. The more we try to be in control of them, the more we find ourselves running a hundred miles an hour but getting nowhere. It seems that the devil's running our lives.

Blame That Lies on Us

We live like mad dogs chasing their own tails. We keep on improving our means of survival and embracing innovation with great pleasure but ignoring the price tag. We're too busy cultivating our gardens to enjoy the harvest. The rich are still as greedy as ever and still trying desperately to protect their wealth.

The middle class has to live large—big, beautiful homes, $70,000 cars, and private schools for their children so they can get into expensive colleges. Juggling too many balls makes it impossible to put on a good show. And the poor, on top of their wounds caused by natural and man-made forces, fall into the poverty of poverty and spend what little they have on drugs, alcohol, and junk food.

Everyone's stressed by the weight on their shoulders but are not letting go of stuff they could live without. Greed and bad behavior have taken over our lives. We've become victims of our greatness. The bad news is that this chaotic train is far from its destination. The younger generation, those who will soon be picking up our torches and running with them, are defaulting on their responsibilities to the detriment of their advancement.

If that all isn't tragic enough, we've been enduring parenting longer than ever as our sons and daughters are seemingly unable to become self-sufficient. They can't and don't want to leave the house before age thirty, and they live as if they've not left. And no matter how hard this reality is, we don't close off their access to us and shouldn't; hell would otherwise be hotter for them.

Life's been demanding that everyone in poor and rich countries alike increase their efforts to meet the new standards of basic life while the means to do that are decreasing. We've bitten off more than we can chew and swallowing it before we should. This is the curse of our time, and we don't seem capable of reversing it. As a result, we're not living because we're too busy trying to live. We're killing ourselves trying to live. We have to push the free riders, annoying passengers, and luggage out of the way to find comfortable seats on the train we're on, and when we reach our destination, we have to contend with those vicious dogs and kick the elephants out of the room.

The paradises in our minds might be no more, but we're not forbidden to build new ones especially now that we're empowered to take control of the wheel of our destiny. We must tackle our problems at the heart and sharpen our fighting tools—education and our finances, our health, diet, exercise, and more instead of simply accepting what others have ready to serve us.

I think you're thinking I'm a lunatic because you're sure that even when we develop the seeds of a good living strategy, we don't find fertile land to plant them. Drug epidemics, domestic violence, identity theft, cyberattacks, crime, government shutdowns, layoffs, and unemployment are some of the nightmares we face while trying to implement our living strategies. We're by no means living when we're too busy trying to live.

To accept your current condition is to let life run you. That philosophy will make you embrace laziness and procrastination, and then you'll be unable to live not because you're too busy trying but because you're busy saving yourself for after death. Donald Trump disrupted the prosperity we were enjoying after 9/11 and up to 2016 just as the coronavirus is doing now. Nonetheless, we're trying to regain control over the train we're on and live happy lives. We should keep that effort going.

19

The Curse of Time

THE WORLD CONTINUES TO ENDURE drastic changes in the shape of calamities and catastrophes. It survived the Ice Age and that asteroid that hit Earth 65 million years ago and drove dinosaurs to extinction, but droughts and floods still wreak havoc, and plagues are still around; we're paying for all that in many ways. Future generations will have to endure distasteful residues of the past on top of the curses of their time.

North Korea keeps testing missiles, and Russia and the US are increasing the number of their nuclear warheads and mobilizing troops. China and the US are about to put gloves on to settle some business matters. Even wars of words and political rhetoric worry us because these two countries have powerful militaries, weaponry, and nuclear bombs and drive the world's economy.

Extension of Malice

We have two kinds of human curses: natural and man-made. Ebola, measles, and mumps have come back to haunt us. Cancer is one of our biological curses. Colds and the flu continue to whip us every winter. Volcanoes erupt, and tornadoes, hurricanes, and tsunamis leave us mad, miserable, and limping economically. Add to all that the human-created curses such as smoking, drinking, relationships, horns of angels of the land, terrorism, and war.

Smoking. We started smoking grass and herbs since we discovered thousands of years ago that these greens were medicine, but today, we either didn't know or don't care that marijuana is addictive and harmful to our health.

Drinking. We started drinking tea from leaves and roots for medicinal purposes, but now, we're losing millions of lives worldwide due to excessive drinking, and we're spending millions fighting alcohol addiction.

Relationships. I don't think we know exactly when our relationships start going bad, but I think it was shortly after their first birthday. It's hard to imagine that relationships, the best life has to offer us, carry malice in their souls. Well, we know every good has a bad riding piggyback and waiting for an opportunity to strike.

The difficulties involved in maintaining relationships and marriages are driving people to stay single longer, but that's no fun. We see the wagon of relationship benevolence speeding away.

The horns of angels of the land. The side effect of every good is monsters hidden under the bed. Science and technology for example are angels that make our lives easier, but they come with hidden horns. We're still celebrating the marriage of science and technology and will continue to do so until death do us part, but we'll also have to deal with those horns.

Terrorism. Terrorism has been with us ever since humanity took root. Fortunately, we learn new tricks to deal with it and its consequences after each strike, but we can count on terrorism existing to the end of time.

Wars. Born with it, grew up in it, and living with it, we'll die and leave war standing strong. Wars of words or weaponry aren't going anywhere.

Natural and man-made curses disrupt our assembly line and slow us down as they have been doing forever, but past generations have survived them. Let us understand our time and embrace sacrifice for the sake of prosperity but never turn our backs on our curses of any kind.

Countries with and in pursuit of nuclear bombs want to have big, powerful dogs to scare intruders away and gain international respect. They'll not dare let those dogs out however because they know everyone else has one. Regardless, nuclear war is a catastrophic threat, and so are terrorist attacks. What we can do is live with our curses and stay focused on becoming empowered, joyful, and excellent. Otherwise, fear, misery, anguish, and suffering will increase our rage against natural and human stupidity.

Joy and happiness don't come from staring at the shadows of beasts in front of you and fearing others to come; they come from what you can achieve in spite of the punches. The harder you prepare for that battle, the easier your victory will be, and you and your descendants will be and stay ahead of the game. You need strength to change what you can, serenity to accept what you can't, and the right to freedom and happiness. You also have the wisdom it takes to live in spite of any curse.

20

Lost in Translation

By the time we can count to ten, we've developed some sense of life and some behavioral norms based on what we were punished for and what we were praised for. We learned at least to respect ourselves and others of all ages, share with our siblings, and study hard.

During adolescence, these lessons were somewhat shaken but not eradicated. We learned that we succeed at work and in our social lives when we treat others with love, care, empathy, and respect. And then we become parents who teach our children the same rules. We tell them, "If you don't do lots of stupid things or take many wrong turns, you'll be fine and will stay ahead of the game." Well, not quite so in recent years. Actually, since many decades ago.

Employers aren't offering jobs to those attending college before they graduate if they're offering jobs at all. Worshiping a god and going to church no longer ensure eternal love, peace, harmony, and brotherhood. In fact, people have been massacred in churches, mosques, temples, and other places of worship. It's worth remembering that these phenomena have been with us all along. Still, forks in the road are more daunting than ever; we can't just close our eyes and pick one. We must make a full stop, think clearly, select a path, and then proceed with caution.

Many of the principles we grew up with have let us down because they became obsolete, uninspiring, or unsuitable. Getting enough sleep, chewing slowly, resting for fifteen minutes after a meal before exercising, and working hard are principles we still implement, but they aren't cutting it anymore. Many people have long commutes to and from work and have to squeeze in shopping, cooking, cleaning, some exercise, and helping their kids with their homework. They watch some TV, check Facebook, catch the evening news—we've become addicted to the last three items—and decide what to wear the next day as well as plan meals for it.

Sure, not everybody needs eight hours of sleep, but the problem is that almost no one is getting the sleep they need and that what sleep they get is not of a good quality. We go to bed late worried about waking up late. Our heads are filled with trash, anger, and frustration. If we don't bounce between nightmares and insomnia, the tossing and turning we do unconsciously take away our ability to have a good night's sleep. And sex gets lost in translation much less celebrated and honored.

Whether or not chewing slowly and resting for fifteen minutes after eating make sense, it's a joke. We eat on the run or at our desks while we work. We rush through meals at home to move on to other tasks and are lucky to not suffer indigestion. Our best-laid plans collapse, and we end up disappointed failures.

We think that the rich are the lucky bastards who got it better than right until we hear their complaints and try to understand their crying and realize those making more than $200,000 a year didn't get it right. So what about everyone else?

From the time society split into three distinct classes, the poor kept their doors open to everyone without racism, discrimination, bias, or prejudice. According to some 2017 statistics, 80 percent of the world's population was in poverty, and the times haven't gotten any better for them, and they fall into the poverty of poverty. Clearly, the poor didn't get it right. Well, somebody must have! What about governments? I'm kidding. Thinking that governments got it right is a laughing-out-loud emoji; governments get it wrong even when they get it right.

I'm sure great minds are working hard to come up with strategies to make life work for all, but so far, they've just been running in circles. The widespread and persistent low tides followed by rough waters have been making swimming through life a nightmare, and our navigational skills are leaving us stranded in the ocean. Principles that worked before aren't working today. We're lost in translation. And that's not a good thing. We must dig deeper into our powers to come up with a formula for success. When we abandon a sinking ship, we don't focus on the reason the ship started sinking; we just swim for shore. We're lost in translation. The old rules are not fitted for our new reality. New times demand fresh, new philosophies coupled with old ones, wisdom, and grit. The flickering lights at the end of the tunnel are the beacons for a reinvention of ourselves.

Reinventing Ourselves

Lucky you! Your ancestors gave you the best genes. Your parents got you to succeed in school, and you got a college degree. There's not a dream of yours that won't come true. Unless you screw up badly, reinventing yourself would be a foolish maneuver. Unfortunately, the rest of us who win sometimes, lose other times, and tie most of the time must reinvent ourselves to stay in the game and get ahead of it, but that's stressful and involves shedding some blood. When we finally become who we thought we were meant to be, we find out how badly we suck at it. Then we take another road out of desperation but find out that it leads nowhere. But one day, like a miracle, we find ourselves on a journey we've always despised, avoided, or never even thought of. Despite all, we should never give up.

When I was ten, I dreamed of becoming a soldier. Years later, I wanted to be a pilot. And then a doctor. My grandparents, who raised me, especially my grandpa, didn't care about what I became as long as I got a higher education. During high school, I was focused on aviation; I chose classes such as geography that fit the purpose. While I was sorting things out, I was employed by one of the largest enterprises in the country, which allowed me to develop my English skills. It was tough at first, but by the end of my first year there, I had progressed. The aviation bug was still biting me and particularly after my work moved closer to the airport; I watched planes landing and taking off all the time. My boss told me, "Go to the US and get your pilot's license, buddy!"

I listened. Sadly, after my retina detached, which happened right after I started taking commercial flying lessons, becoming a pilot began to show its ugly, daunting face of impossibility. The dream was fading. I wondered, *Now what?*

For better or worse, I never liked literature, but I loved to read and write. That passion kept my brain busy. After having tried a few paths to making it big (including a venture into environmental services that faced impossible obstacles post-9/11), I was dissatisfied with my life. I wanted to become a lawyer, but law school wasn't quite my thing. I took a correspondence business course and got a diploma in business management, but I was still dazed and confused as to a career. Destiny slapped me hard; it gave me pen and paper and ordered me to write. A few years later, I published my first book, volume 1 of the trilogy *Stay Ahead of the Game.* (Beginning of story.)

Many geniuses, famous people, stars, and even landscapers and farmers started off on tough paths but continued on them until destiny showed up and changed their course. Tom Cruise is an example. After spending years in the seminary, he become one of the most highly paid actors. This is to say that sometimes, it's easy to believe that our journey is written in the books and that if we neglect to find our true passion, destiny will put it in our path. And yet, it's always better to get there by ourselves.

Be wise enough to understand your gifts and passions, and be sure you're on the right track. At the first sign of doubt and uncertainty, reinvent yourself especially when you're unsatisfied with your achievements and progress.

Reinventing yourself does not mean a gender change or walking on your hands rather than your feet. Reinventing yourself means embracing different philosophies and principles of life some of which you might have been despising. It also means freeing yourself of your mental shackles, giving a new dynamic to your assembly line by replacing sections of it with new parts. Health, nutrition, and fitness could be a good place to start. You might have to do some things including the following.

Change your culture of drugs. Reduce visits to drug stores, hospitals, and doctors' offices for minor headaches, stomach pains, back pains, sore muscles, scrapes, swelling, and so on. Give your immune system a chance to do what it's supposed to do—fight bugs and heal your injuries.

Change your food culture. Pizza, cheeseburgers, fried chicken, junk food, concentrated juices, and sugary drinks might need to be swapped out for beans, cereals, fruits, broccoli, lettuce, kale, and other healthy foods.

Change your hobbies. Switch off the TV and hit the gym.

Consider your personality. Your personality could be your worst enemy, so diagnose it to find areas in need of improvement and find areas that you should quarantine. Embrace a strategy that empowers you to reach new heights. Avoid trouble with the law at all costs; a criminal record can leave you with just about a zero chance of getting a job. A personality that smells trouble miles away must be cleansed and tamed at all costs because the consequences stink. And if you're blessed with a great personality, streamline it in accordance with your dreams and goals.

Education. Higher education has become a necessity albeit an expensive necessity. If you stop your education at the high school level and quit learning simply because you want to avoid nightmares, you'll be tackled by worse nightmares and face uglier monsters that could drive you all the way down to the poverty of poverty. You want to do something other than flipping burgers. Get some fuel in your train of success by pursuing a higher education; don't wait until you get home and find your belongings in a bag because your mom is fed up with supporting a thirty-nine-year-old, irresponsible, and unappreciative son who lives in the basement. Reinvent yourself.

Friends, society, and yourself. Our friendships are social circles that prepare us for society as the rules governing friendship are similar to those of society. We follow such rules instinctively to be good friends and integrate into society. In the meantime, social rules can be strong impediments to our advancement, and breaking them can become necessary.

Breaking rules doesn't mean becoming an eccentric outcast; it means being in a crowd but marching toward your own goals and preferably rapidly. Choose whatever is helpful for your cause, and leave the junk behind. If you don't have the strength and endurance to move mountains, remove as many small rocks as you can and use experience to move the bigger ones when you can. In the end, your project could shine better than those who moved mountains by forbidden ways. Distinguish yourself in the crowd, get ahead of the game, reach your goals, and become a true masterpiece. That's reinventing yourself.

Finances and lifestyle. Now more than ever, we must honor the glory that comes from the sweat of our brows.

The time has come to demolish our shacks and build strong fortresses from scratch. That requires money, and money needs to be managed wisely; that means budgeting, earning as much as we can, and spending as little as possible. Our lifestyles must fit our income, and that might mean cutting down on shopping, going to the movies, and not offering to buy everyone a round unless that's reciprocated.

If weed, cigarettes, drugs, and alcohol are your remedies for stress, frustration, and depression, it's time to seek help. You might have to cut down on buying expensive gifts for others and buying five cups of coffee a day. Inspecting your assembly line for determining useless parts is mandatory.

Relationships. A good tango depends on the abilities of the dancers and their commitment to putting on a good show especially when the tango song sucks or the record is scratched. Don't be victimized by relationships. Make a flight plan in detail and follow it.

Stress management. Stress management is mandatory for reinventing yourself and keeping yourself focused on that.

Retirement. It doesn't seem logical for retired people to reinvent themselves; they ought to engage in what brings them pleasure and happiness. Perhaps their state of health limits their ability to do what they used to do—maybe golfing or volunteering as a way to pass on to others the benefits of their life experiences and knowledge. One way or another, they should be active.

The dynamics of our lives are powered by our 37 trillion cells working all the time under all conditions. We contribute just a bit to that long and complicated assembly line with a crazy chain reaction by our determination to make our dreams come true. Let's take job well done by our cells as an inspiration for reinventing ourselves and achieving our maximum potential. This task is hard as can be, but once we understand the game and build our confidence and determination, strength and endurance will follow.

The following should be your constant reminder that

> you wait not to be served a drink; you find lemons, water, and sugar to make lemonade to quench your thirst,
> you catch your own fish,
> you see no evil through the devil's eyes,
> you bear the emblem "Not because it's easy. Because it's hard,"
> you feel no pain because you're focused on the gain,
> he who refuses to see, hear, and speak is blind, deaf, and mute,
> there's no easier said than done, just whatever it takes, and
> unlike losers who come up with excuses, you set goals because you're a winner.

Reinventing yourself can be fun, and it's definitely rewarding. Reinventing yourself could be your best and perhaps only option to avoid living forever lost in translation. Whatever situation you find yourself in, always enjoy the moments life gives you because you grow fast and time flies.

21

Fountain of Grace

We're born with the tools necessary for making our journey safe and sound. We need only the nurturing and support of our parents until we're seventeen or eighteen, when we can take care of our business supposedly and for the most part.

But many of us turned out to be very weak and got lost on the journey due to excessive care and protection. That results in nineteen-year-old girls who know jack about cooking, cleaning house, and caring for babies and twenty-three-year-old guys who don't know how to fry an egg or make a cup of tea. Their survival skills didn't develop. The bombardment of technology and ferocious fights between technology giants to take control of our lives and dominate our inspiration and critical thinking don't help matters.

On top of that, children aren't getting enough nurturing from their parents. If they are, it's of poor quality. They'll be taking care of their parents eventually, that is, if they end up with the resources to do that. Luckily, it doesn't matter how lost and desperate we are; we're surrounded by beacons. Churches, schools, parents, brothers and sisters, and particularly grandmas and grandpas are some of brightest beacons flashing for us. The following helping hands are as important as the beacons are.

Education. Once you earn a higher education degree and keep learning, you can fill your sack of experience with great tools to help you reach the finish line. In case higher education is out of your league or you have no desire to face its nightmares, you can still enrich your education with free online courses and educational materials. There's no such thing as too complicated of a dish that you can't find step-by-step recipes for.

Reading empowering materials may not get you a diploma, but it will open your mind and keep your learning cells busy. It develops your vocabulary, improves your grammar, and reduces memory loss. A stable life depends on economic power and most important on the ability to manage such power. Once you're addicted to learning, you won't need a business degree to manage your finances.

Friends. Once you have great friends, you're on the way to becoming a success. Don't be shy about using your friends' expertise or asking them for advice. Friends are willing to help when asked.

Siblings. Don't think your younger brothers and sisters don't have much to offer. They can be full of inspiration, and that can inspire you to reach out to your power within.

You might work harder to help your little brothers and sisters expand their gifts and ease their pain and suffering, but in the end, you'll better yourself too.

Stars. It's great to worship stars for the inspiration and joy they provide, but it's better to learn their stories, which are far from rosy. To know their pain and sacrifices is to be inspired and empowered to endure your journey; take nothing for granted, and accept nothing but success.

Up close and personal. Your family is a fountain of grace, and a family of your own is the gold mine. Your children are not just proof of your contribution to the family tree; they're your greatest fountain of grace. Keep them in your heart and mind every second, and commit yourself to overcoming any obstacle to ensure they'll be successful. And keep in mind that the success of your children reflects on your success.

So far, we've traveled to happy places for our inspiration; they're lights in the abyss. Children going to bed on empty stomachs and dying of starvation, young adults whose futures were destroyed by wars and other barbaric acts, young girls forced to marry for economic gain and honor of tradition and taboos, women stoned to death for infidelity, homeless veterans battling PTSD, and elderly being forsaken in nursing homes make up a picture of drama any of us could be forced to face and endure. Take a close look at it and do whatever it takes to ensure that you and yours don't see yourselves in that picture.

We're standing here because we won the sperm race. Life gets more complicated as we age as do the means for achieving our goals. All the negatives out there can make us feel like losers, but that's only if we allow that. Our weaponry for fighting the beasts of life can be useless if we don't use them. If we see no beacons of inspiration around us, we can open our package and search for the tools we need. If clouds and darkness obstruct our path, we can let the stars in us shine brighter.

Anyone preaching that we're living in times of glory and prosperity hassle free is a lunatic. Those surrendering to deception and desperation have either forgotten their mission on earth or have lost the core of their souls, the invincible warriors in them.

My heart is speared and my eyes shed tears every time I see young and powerful minds heading toward failure because they're incapable of appreciating their existence and acting on their power and grace. They've surrendered their souls to the devils that have been preaching disempowering sermons and guiding them to the abyss. These young, powerful minds are treasures, comforts, guardian angels, and pain relievers we've been longing for, but they can't deliver. Let's all wake up and smell the roses! The roads ahead will have many bumps, but we can't just turn around and go home.

We're surrounded by forces opposing our advancement to excellence because our excellence means the elimination of players who cheat. Powerful minds are in almost total control of the games and our success. They watch our moves carefully and are always ready to chop off our wings. The opposing forces they control make fountains of grace look like sleeping dogs. Lots of vicious action takes place behind the scenes; that's what makes our opposition powerful. Well, we're not so bad ourselves. We can easily defeat them with a good strategy. We have what it takes to control our destinies. It's easier when we read between the lines and fill in the blanks, for when we do, we will see fountains of grace and not be scared.

I suggest that young boys watch *Top Gun*, starring Tom Cruise. We need those vibes back. And I tell young girls to pick up the pace of their quest to show men their superiority.

22

Slippery Roads

WE FREQUENTLY HEAR ABOUT SOMEONE who was been beaten up or killed for cheating and stealing and others who overdosed on drugs. People can become victims of the slippery roads they choose to take. Other times, our victimization is the fault of others and things we have no control over. Here are some examples.

Realtors can be just waiting for people with bad credit to come along and convince them to apply for mortgages anyway. When the housing bubble burst in 2008, the entire world suffered the consequences and many people lost the houses they were tricked into buying.

Others will try to tempt us with drugs hoping to get us hooked and come back to them for more. They're devils seducing us with sugar. Tobacco companies want to hook teens on cigarettes and have them buying their products forever.

Girls go through the same puberty battles boys do except to a greater extent because, well, they're females who were created with greater capacities for loving, caring, and nurturing. They can fall for good looks, swagger, and hypnotizing love and become teen moms. Boys on the contrary go for numbers, which should be a clue for girls.

Girls and boys can become victims of slip-and-falls in the land of love. At that age, it's almost impossible to be rational. The urge to venture into new territories doesn't help either. Cheating comes from the desire to have sex in forbidden lands, but that could lead to separation and divorce and the crumbling of our relationship castle. Just the other day, I watched a Facebook video of a man beating his wife in the jungle when he caught her cheating. Despite social changes and evolution, unfaithfulness continues to be a bloodstain on a white dress and bird poop on a man's hat.

The journey of life has all kinds of slippery roads with dangerous slopes, and it's just about impossible not to fall and twist an ankle or break a leg. Being cautious helps, but still, some injuries are just the cost of doing business. Get up, walk on safe parts of the road, and be better prepared for your next slips, trips, and falls. Don't bury your head in the sand with your ass exposed. Most important, don't gather your shame, pain, and suffering and then evaporate on your trek to excellence.

Salvador and his two best friends were inspiring teenagers until they were expelled from the seminary for having escaped the facility to attend a concert in town. One became a great musician and another a great English teacher. Salvador, on the other hand, faced harder times; his job in social services allowed him to embezzle money for years, but then he was caught and went to prison for it. After serving his time, he started drinking again and avoiding his friends and family. Everyone wanted to help him, but no one knew where he was. He died at age forty-one.

It doesn't matter how you got yourself sidetracked in life; you can always fight harder and achieve your goals. Life's filled with roses and thorns, beauties and beasts. You won't get to travel in great weather and cherish laughter without sacrifice, so never give up on your quest for happiness simply because life has thrown you into an abyss. Get up, dust yourself off, and get going.

Youngsters, beware of taking a year off after high school to decide what you want to do with your life. This is the most dangerous spot on the slippery road toward education, so avoid it at all costs.

23

Future to the Past

WHEN WE TALK ABOUT THE future, we're talking about the days and nights ahead. We want them to be filled with prosperity and happiness, but they can be spooky due to the ugly shadows of yesterday and today. Worst of all, we're living days ahead every day. We're so busy dealing with the demands of today that we can't think of the days ahead. Since we want to do better, let's talk about the future to the past to see if there's light at the end of tunnel.

The future to the past allows us to understand the dynamics of past days, weeks, months, years, decades, centuries, and millennia with their achievements that made our lives better as well as the atrocities whose consequences we're still dealing with. On the other hand, it helps us understand the mysteries of our lives and gather clues to predict tomorrow.

Crimes and despicable actions of horror and shame were committed in the past—the holocaust and slavery for instance. Some empires fell, and others rose. Nations screwed each other up, and nations became friends. Friends turned into foes, and foes became friends. Poverty, crime, divorce, social injustice, vandalism, and a whole long list of other social and natural catastrophes are characters in history.

The past improved, innovated, and reached outstanding goals that enabled us to see the future not as doomsdays to come but as a continuation of realities with better ingredients. The trouble is that despite our forward movement, the road is taking us back to where we came from. The surroundings are new, but the destination is old. The actors are different, but the play is the same.

Sadly, science and technology share the blame with governments and other agents for our current predicament. We can order things online while seated on our couches, pay less than we would have at a store, and get them delivered in no time. But that's all at the expense of human contact and being active; we prefer to stay lazy and isolated.

GPS—the greatest navigation tool yet—is increasingly more reliable, accurate, and easier to use, but it severely hinders our navigational skills and need to ask others for directions; it's another drop in the antisocial bucket.

And forget watching a game with your buddies; you can watch it on your smartphone anywhere you want alone. And talking with others has devolved into simply texting them. We're congregating with smaller and smaller circles of individuals; it's back to the caves of Africa or Mars.

How could the richest 1 percent of society be the dominant class? But it is, and their wealth is flowing behind the scenes to their favorite politicians. The filthy rich are making it tough for the middle class and making the poor even poorer.

Worthless Coin or a Treasure?

Nothing can stop us now! Curiosity flowed freely in the past, is flowing freely today, and will be flowing freely forever because curiosity killed the cat and the rest spread the disease. Then we believed that necessity was the mother of all inventions; for that, we invented necessity. Sex is great, and babies are angels, so we overpopulated the world, which created more necessity. More necessity, more invention … Remember?

Then we realized that speed was an awesome thing. (Yeah, I'm guilty as charged. I dreamed of flying a shuttle to the moon.) Many things have sped up time and made us live in a rush to improve quickly. We're down to designer babies and gene editing, and we'll be interacting with cyborgs pretty soon. It seems that God retired and allowed his best creation to take over, except like an idiot, man is creating his own replacement—stupidity at its best. Small brains can do nothing other than cuss out money and big brains.

From this perspective, a trip to the past to see the future is worthless. We see nothing to excite us, and we aren't thrilled to meet what's driving us insane. If we don't see the future through pessimistic and foggy lenses, the future will take us back to the caves if it doesn't make us extinct. Even if this threat's real, worrying about it is disempowering.

The future to the past is an imaginary trip we should take to empower ourselves in the present for the sake of the future. In that sense, the future to the past is a treasure. We look back to see our past dark paths and get flashlights; we see the weakest links of our ancestors and prepare ourselves for what might come.

Don't allow yourself to be consumed by the chaos of today or the fear of tomorrow. Find inspiration in the future to the past and have a brilliant future. Even if forward movement takes us back to the caves of Africa, we won't have to fear a thing as long as we stay ahead of the game.

Our trip back to the caves could mean a trip to different caves. We've gone to the moon several times. We've been wandering and studying the universes with the help of robots. We're now in the process of visiting and colonizing Mars. This is where the reverse trip's taking us. The human quest is infinite. When our offspring celebrate humankind's billionth year, we'll be part of the ceremony. We should contribute now to the celebration to come. Simply because we won't be present for it is no reason to turn our backs and go home. The future to the past is forward movement toward darkness only if we allow it to be. We can empower ourselves to live happily wherever time takes us.

I was speaking to Peter, a friend of mine, about technology's fast evolution, and he said, "I'm glad I'm gonna die soon. I don't wanna see all the scary shit that's coming." But that scary shit doesn't scare me much less make me want to die soon. I can't wait to enjoy it.

For a better understanding of the benefits of the future to the past, adopt a competitive attitude toward your past to achieve excellence in the future. Reflect on your situation and conditions years ago and vow to do better even if you're on top of your game today. Make more trips to the future to the past, and prepare to indulge in the goodies it'll bring.

Back to the future is taking us to unknown territories where the wonders are infinite and we will be God—at least until man no longer exists. Space is still expanding, but so is our ability to learn more about it. We know earth will no longer exist one day millions of years from now assuming many other things that could destroy it remain dormant. Since we don't want to become extinct just yet, we're rushing to make it to Mars and save humankind. At least this is how it all stands; reading between the lines and filling in the blanks allow us to see well into the beyond.

Mars is our first choice, but we'll search for other livable planets, and robots will help us with that. Science will evolve, take gene editing up to an elite level, and give us a new species to be our representatives far beyond Mars. If our offspring, enhanced by gene editing and with the assistance of computer chips, don't overtake artificial intelligence, man will create something that can do that. Depending on what's abundant in space—radiation and dark matter come to mind—the new we will live much easier lives; no bones and flesh will mean no need for food and drink. Dark matter will no longer be dark to us; it could be what we need to spread throughout space. If Earth and Mars are still around, they'll be nothing but big junkyards. And we'll consider it mind-boggling that Earth is where life appeared and evolved to what we are now but wonder how modern humans were the smartest creatures of all Earth's creatures then.

Will the new we—the fruits of our creation, not human evolution and thus carrying none or very little of a humankind signature—be our offspring? I believe our signature is immortal, and so we'll be racing against super artificial intelligence. I also believe we'll win the race sometimes but lose most of the time. And if we stay as an inferior power in our space and mind our own business, super artificial intelligence will leave us alone. And we'll make friends with many of them for our continued prosperity and continuity.

My belief comes from the fact that God gave us modern humans all the keys to the specie's continuity and then retired. We might not be able to save all other species, but we will last until all of space dies. Let's enjoy ourselves as much as we can; we were chosen to do that.

The new we won't have any emotions; that means no crying, madness, stress, frustration, desires, or anxiety. And the tragic thing is that sex will no longer exist. As a result, no bloodshed over penises and vaginas or stoning adulterers thank God. Life will be driven by love, peace, brotherhood, and harmony. Great? Great! Life with no parenting nightmares, traffic jams, and jerks and idiots on the roads… No drugs, alcohol, cigarettes, laws, politicians, or cops… No wars, immigration, racism, or discrimination… No poverty… Nobody dying of hunger… No inability to get a higher education… No battles over inheritances. But wait… All those things make life mysterious and interesting. How could we (they) live without them? If life sucks now, imagine how it'll be a billion years from now without all the above. We won't like it, but we won't have to.

As we prepare to conquer space, we become more enslaved by technology, which is killing us little by little. You youngsters are being used as the main driver of that though you don't know that. You're being used as the means for the transitions to come and for the obliteration of what we have now.

We have no doubts we'll bring video games and online activities for social interaction and entertainment to other planets, but we don't want you to give in so easily. To honor our resistance to whatever is unsure, at least enjoy all that's available to you. You might be comfortable in your living room playing video games with your online friends, but remember to nurture and soothe your souls, something nothing can do better than nature. Our bond with nature is ingrained in our DNA. Parks, lakes, rivers, bushes, jungles, and forests are still welcoming you. They like to see you and talk to you. Outdoor activity is easy and healthy for everyone. The future to the past is demanding all of us and especially you youngsters to enjoy what's still good in nature, your best friend. Machines, toys, robots, and artificial intelligence are friends as well that you can unite with nature and use the resulting power for your benefit. Your contribution to human evolution will go far beyond your journey's end.

Geniuses are still intrigued about the origin of life, and I don't think they'll ever discover it, but I don't care and neither should you. What's clear is that the future to the past allows us to understand the changes of yesterday and today and predict the changes of tomorrow.

Let's all live and let others live in ways that will make the future a better place all the way to the end of time. Our lifestyles today should be better than those of yesterday and should inspire tomorrow's. The good seeds we plant now can produce delicious fruit forever.

24

Miscellaneous

We all want to become big winners, but that depends on many factors such as our ancestors, threats and opportunities, culture, tradition, philosophy, our commitment to sacrifice, and most important, how extensive our assembly line is and how smoothly it runs.

The rich live large—mansions, yachts, private jets. The middle class live large too in their own way—nice houses, families, friends. But those in both classes worry about losing what they have. Their assembly lines might be long, but they have to be tended to or there will be problems.

People lose jobs for many reasons, some of which they are responsible for. Those who are poorly educated are always in trouble because they lack the brainpower to properly care for the basics of life. If we get good-paying jobs but spend like crazy, we'll go broke. If we marry our high school sweethearts but neglect the small but important details of marriage, we could end up miserable. If we don't repair leaky faucets, we could flood our homes. If we wear cheap shoes, we could end up with back pain and creaky knees. We should never forget that the big picture is made up of many small ones that we need to pay attention to. They're the ingredients of our dishes, the foundations of our castles, the roots of our strong, tall trees. We can't live our lives flawlessly; we're human, and the world is crazy. But we can take care of our responsibilities big and small.

As we grow older, our assembly line expands and miscellaneous factors increase in number as do our responsibilities. One small neglect can trigger a bad chain reaction on our assembly line. Not getting an education will cause our finances to suck, and we'll learn that poverty sucks too. If we neglect our health by using drugs, alcohol, and cigarettes, that can lead to the poverty of poverty, and stress and frustration will party in us day and night for as long as we live. We'll be on our deathbeds alone except for all our regrets. Not a pretty picture. Not a nice ending.

Prepare for the inevitable challenges of life, and make the sacrifices necessary to keep your assembly line running. Every penny counts. Every small detail matters. Every small opportunity should be grabbed. At the end of the game, you'll be the soothsayer who got it right, and that will feel great.

We can't leave this chapter without touching two giants of life we give little attention to—sleep and stress—though we've dealt with them before.

We know that getting enough sleep is important for so many reasons physical and mental if we want to keep our assembly lines running smoothly, but if we neglect our need for sleep and particularly good-quality sleep, we'll invite stress into the room. The problem is that we don't pay attention to what we're not paying attention to. The consequences of that are numerous and spread all over the apparatus of our lives.

At work, we won't be able to focus. While driving, we'll experience road rage. Our other responsibilities will overwhelm us. We'll become depressed and frustrated. And it's all a vicious cycle as lack of sleep produces more stress, which causes more lack of sleep. We humans are simply too smart for ourselves.

Everybody should figure out how to restore order in their courtrooms; they can pound the gavel at their lack of sleep and then at whatever is stressing them out or vice versa, but they ultimately have to deal with both if they want to regain and retain peace of mind.

Let's give sleep and stress management the attention they deserve because they're elements of our assembly line. Let us not say, "It is what it is." We can adjust our priorities and rearrange our daily obligations to get the amount and quality of sleep we need and to cut down on stress, which affects our ability to get that sleep. Neglecting either one is detrimental to our health and advancement. Neglecting both is a knockout punch.

When you lose sleep, find ways to compensate for that by sleeping longer on the weekend, not five weeks from now, or it could become too late to regain your loss.

25

Staying in Touch and Closer

We're living in a time of ample opportunities to make any dream come true. Even in developing countries, this sentiment is alive and well as cooperation among nations brings many benefits for all. In rich countries, saying, "If you can think it, you can do it," is true, but the rate and amplitude of individuals' successes are not matching the opportunities at their disposal. This picture is not pretty let alone perfect with youngsters moving into adulthood completely off track and lacking the determination to stand up to challenges. Something's definitely off here, and I see two troublemakers: technology and government.

Don't get mad at me just yet for blaming technology and government for everything wrong with the world; I have my reasons, and I'll give them to you. They are the two most important agents dumping distractions on us 24/7 that intentionally or not keep us unfocused. Ever since the sixties, the wagon of technology has been moving faster and faster and has created more and more. Unfortunately, the dust is thicker on the gravel roads that most people travel, and that dust blocks our vision and slows us down. We roll up our windows and proceed with caution.

The wagon of technology creates tons of distractions that keep us hooked and out of touch with our projects. It's also made the world an even noisier place. The only way we can have peace and tranquility is by wearing headsets, but we must shrink our playlists or we won't have time to listen to our favorite tunes.

Government leaves us stranded and pissed off with its laws, rules, and regulations. To be fair, other things cause us to stray from our projects, but listing them all is nearly impossible. And technology and government aren't exactly pointing guns at our heads to bump us off the road to excellence. On the contrary; they're the two main characters in our story, the fastest wagons to take us to our destination—ahead of the game in love, peace, harmony, security, and confidence.

In countries with minimal technology and corrupt governments, people have just about zero possibilities for growth much less success. But the side effects of robust technology and even a good government can hurt us.

We're the greatest obstacles to our success particularly when we waste time. We procrastinate when we should be acting. We slow down when we should speed up. We engage in activities that work to our detriment; playing video games comes to mind. We have to strike a balance between work and pleasure by prioritizing our activities because the demands on us only become heavier as we age. Our responsibilities demand time that at times we don't have, but that means we must find it. Even if we're progressing, we can do better.

The hands of those crafting the technological toys that make our lives easier might not know about their side effects or might just not care about them; they've hit the sweet spot they'd been searching for. And governments have to do whatever is necessary, but so can we. The more we engage in games created by others, the more we hurt our own game. Our dreams won't see sunshine unless we make that our priority.

We can make our game interesting by staying in close contact with our means of progressing. We can protect our dreams and projects by keeping our eyes and ears open as do the shining stars and the big shots.

Life's always playing new games and increasing the weight of our responsibilities on our shoulders as it whisks away the meals and drinks we need for strength, endurance, and growth. This reality pushes us away from our daily responsibilities.

Had you been my siblings, our father would have been of great help to you. He lives back home, Cape Verde Islands, with my mom and the rest of the family. I try to call them at least once a month though they want me to call more often than that. My father keeps me up to date on family matters and his neighbors. It's his way of telling me that I should stay in close contact with my family. In the same way, you can stay in close contact with the apparatus of your life and prioritize it.

Our education, jobs, finances, and relationships all call for our attention. Our goals and dreams are crying for our presence, but we don't seem to hear them, and that's a sin we should repent for.

Once you embrace your projects daily, inspiration comes to fuel your Jaguar that will overtake all the wagons in front of you. Take your projects and dreams with you everywhere, and go to bed with them on your mind. Rest assured that you'll shine brighter.

To feel the warmth and heartbeat of life, you have to hug it and never let go.

26

It Isn't What It Seems

THE MEMBERS OF OUR FAMILIES individually and collectively defend each other, and our friends do the same. When I was a child, my neighborhood was filled with families that had children carrying diseases and abnormalities who were kept out of sight. Our elders told us whom we should stay away from such as witches, despicable young adults, and a few old people considered a danger to children. Now, since I'm not a kid anymore, my parents don't hide secrets from me; they've confirmed my assumptions about a person or two whom I'd thought of as weird back in the day.

A few families in our village had flawless images that they maintained at all cost. They were churchgoers and were respected by others. One family had a daughter who suffered from brain damage; they kept her out of sight as much as possible. Even today, she's not allowed to leave the house, and she's kept out of sight when visitors come.

Once when I was home on vacation, she brought tears to my eyes not because she had missed me but because I had missed her. We had played with each other when we were children despite her being seven years older. She told me through her body language that despite her chopped wings, she would fly if it weren't for being hidden away.

Her family kept our conversation tight and to the point as if there was something to hide. And there was. I later found out that my friend's condition had deteriorated. Frankly, I hadn't noticed any changes—maybe my compassion had blocked my brain's sight—but whatever she had been suffering from (my mom thought she might have been schizophrenic) had gotten worse. Her parents kept her out of sight to uphold the family's reputation, but that was at the expense of her freedom. People go to extremes to hide their flaws and protect their images.

My friend John Doe 12 got into a car accident. His insurance coverage allowed for a rental up to $30 a day. He paid an additional $27 a day to rent a nicer car. He was riding in town showing it off as his own new car. We spend $450 on an outfit, borrow our friend's Mercedes, BMW, and go to the fanciest restaurants in town for a date. We post only the best selfies and vacation videos, we show off our houses and hope people don't find out that the down payment came from an illicit claim of a car accident or a payoff from a legitimate medical error and that we're having a hard time paying the mortgage. This malice seems to act like a cancer; it spreads fast until the victims are dead.

Critical Thinking

Sure, it's great and empowering to behold what others do to better themselves, but it's foolish and sinful to live by what people have or by what we watch, hear, and read without filtering the lies out of the truth. In fact, even when the truth is as good as it can get, if we don't read between the lines and fill in the blanks, we'll get only half-truths. Critical thinking has the power to bring out the whole truth. It also takes us to black-and-white lands and later to gray lands to show us how dinner's cooked and see what's in it. There, we realize some things.

We hear 90 percent bad news and 10 percent good news because bad news is what sells. Powerful news organizations mold stories to fit their purpose—increased ratings and sales. Every story—real and fake—is boiled up or watered down according to a set of objectives rather than the truth of the matter. The good part of a story might not make it due to time restrictions or simply because some big donors would be hurt by it. Sure, truth matters… just at its little corner desk. Investigative journalism and real news are being left behind and discredited by the hectic overflow of online information chasing us 24/7 as if we're rabbits for dinner.

China and other countries have the most jaw-dropping airports, malls, and skyscrapers. As of 2018, China is second-largest economy in the world—soon to become number one—and with unmatched annual growth. China's swift rise to superpower status is seen and felt around the world. Some people predict that China will steal the all-time North Star status from the US. This has been an ongoing story for decades. The problem is stories of this kind fail to mention that China is rising from the US's platform and yet there are people who may be living there on $1 a day and people there can talk and write only in the language of the government or be sent to jail. Some days, people have to wear masks or die of air pollutants. Wealthy Chinese move their money to the US, and some go there to have babies who will then be US citizens and then return home.

The US dollar is the number one international currency, and the US's military budget continues to be larger than that of the rest of world combined. People around the world dream about moving to the land of the free and the home of the brave. English is on the fast track to becoming the official language of planet Earth. It seems that for better or worse, the US has been granted by the gods, aliens, and grit the power to lead world; other countries have a long road ahead to catch up let alone get ahead of it. China deserves hats off for being a great player that's risen from ashes to become an MVP and has achieved many great milestones. No country's as beautiful, powerful, and prosperous as it seems, nor are any as draconian as some believe.

We can go on forever with beautiful but fake realities because we fail to think outside the box. Before we praise the beauty in front of us and curse the beasts in our path, we should use our critical thinking abilities to reason with our surroundings and stay ahead of the game. Nothing can empower us more than thinking outside the box.

Drift away from the main stories you hear. Construct your full story free of bias, and remember that the more you understand the origin and development of knowledge, the less likely you'll be fooled or enraged by it. Just as in every fairy tale there's a monster to scare the children, big lies about the truth are in front of you, and crimes are behind others' treasures. A monkey in a suit is still a monkey. If it looks too good to be true, it probably is.

Current times have made us live out in the open. We post just about everything we do. Why do we go through so much trouble to avoid the impossible? Well, that's the exact reason we should chill out and reflect on this very crowded world affecting us in two ways. We waste time when we check out all that we see and hear, and we believe everything we see and then feel like underdogs. As a result, we fight to measure up while our means to achieve that are slim to none, and that frustrates us. Suddenly, we're not living our lives for ourselves; we're living the fake lives of others. We jump into the water because everyone else is, and then we return home sick because the water was freezing. We should test the water first.

27

Biological Flaws

Forget biology; it's too flawed. I'm going to reveal my findings about that. You're probably thinking I'm going to remind you of the long journey that started 14 billion years ago and passed many milestones up to our being the ultimate product of God's creation or the finest product of evolution. Unfortunately, I don't have time for that now. I do have time, though, to give you reasons that biology is flawed and how we can cope with that and live happily ever after.

Ages of Turbulence

Along with puberty comes behaviors that can have regrettable consequences including the loss of the love of our parents and family members. We all have regrettable memories of our teen years and don't know why we did what we did. Those who entered adulthood limping, handicapped, or alive but not living thanks to the curses of puberty are the true victims.

Teenagers of all genders are serving time for their crimes, but luckily, the laws of the land understand the internal turbulence teenagers go through and tend to give them breaks until they really screw up. As adults, they're ashamed, frustrated, and full of regrets. Their despicable actions put them where they are now because biology was running the show on stage and behind the scenes.

Sexual Decline

There's no denying that sex is the best gift of life. So why do males hit sexual peaks at age eighteen and females hit them after age thirty? Why do so many things make Johnny too sleepy to enter the house of party? And then more often than not, every time there's a party, men are done before women. What's up with that?

As males age, their testosterone levels go down. This weakness starts at about age forty-five, but their need for sex increases. The mind says yes, but the body says no. Sex has tons of health benefits. As we get older, our stressors increase, and that causes a need for more sex, but if Johnny refuses to party or our partners are dealing with menopause or a disinterest in sex—a libido decline—we could lose opportunities to establish emotional balance through sex. With the exception of a few bad actions of ours such as drinking, smoking, and doing drugs, males' erectile dysfunction and females' libido decline are as far as I can see the fault of biology.

Elderly Dependence

As we age, our need for independence increases while the means to stay independent decrease. Our motor skills become weaker. Our senses become impaired. Diseases and conditions such as Alzheimer's can attack us unmercifully and leave us at the mercy of technology and family members. I see no biological perfection here.

Longevity

We know that our genes govern how long we live. Good health due to advances in medicine helps us live happier and longer. By the time we die, we'll have accumulated enough experience to rock life as no one can and contribute to humanity's excellence. Can you imagine what Einstein, Galileo, da Vinci, Raphael, Michael Faraday, Michelangelo, Dickens, Aristotle, and so many other intelligent people could have brought to humanity if they'd lived a hundred years? Some brains should never get old and die. On the other side of the river, those born with mental illnesses, disabilities, and other biological flaws want to die to end their anguish and pain but live for decades. I see no one or nothing to blame but biology.

Dying in Pain and Suffering

Different philosophies have different explanations for why we die in pain and suffering. I think we're simply too stupid to understand life and death. But frankly, nothing matters much when we're in pain and see death staring at us. We do what it takes to live healthy, happy, and long lives. We avoid injuries and sickness because they cause pain and stop us from enjoying life. When we reach our seventies—much earlier for many—everything we do brings pain and suffering, and that drives us to pills and their side effects. Some take their lives because they didn't accept their biological flaws or gave up the struggle.

However, we must cope with our flaws and enjoy life as we are instead of as we wish we were. No one is a masterpiece. Biological flaws are part of who we are. Some of us may be lucky enough that our flaws don't wake up to taunt us—a good thing—but they can come out of their comas and make us miserable. Whether we're cursed by apparent or hidden flaws, our happiness is something only we can define and find.

We see true testimonies of happiness alive and well in the land of extreme biological flaws. The flawed find ways to thrive and stay ahead of the game, and so can we. We tackle biological and man-made flaws for joy and excitement. Where would the challenge be, and why would we need medicine if we were flawless creatures? What excitement would be in that?

We are all flawed, but we all can exercise our powers to mitigate our flaws. We get glasses, have plastic surgery, buy hearing aids, and go on to enjoy life. Contrary to what I said at the beginning of this subchapter, we're not too stupid to understand life, but we could let stupidity stop us from living happily, so let's not do that.

We have discussed the importance of learning as much as we can about our ancestors to discover our potential and weak links so we can achieve great things. If our ancestors had bad hearts, cancer, diabetes, arthritis, or other inheritable conditions or tendencies, we can take steps to avoid that.

Biological flaws can be death sentences only if we let them be.

28

Players and the Mission

The way events of the world have been unfolding and the speed at which the means for our prosperity have been scattered make it easy for us to think that only a few good men make up the team, but that's not true. We are all human beings in the same game of life. We're similar but not identical; we're all players but with different skills. We won't all be MVPs, but we can all contribute to the team.

Our wishes and desires are prompted by our personalities, environments, threats, and opportunities. We all want to be happy, rich, and famous and have happier, richer, and more-famous kids; that's all ingrained in our DNA.

We are responsible for doing what we can for the good of the team. We're better winners when we combine our wishes and desires with those of the team. We should take three very important and tricky agents of a human being on a quest to excellence: easy, hard, and overconfident. The reason is that more often than we think, they bring us nasty surprises.

Easy Is Hard and Deceiving

In high school one day, I was about to take an important oral quiz in English. Everyone was nervous about it, which was normal. Afterward, people were saying, "I killed it!" or "I nailed it!" or "That was as easy as drinking a glass of water!" (Yes, we say that in Cape Verde too.)

A week later came the moment of truth. Almost the entire class had failed. Even the best student among us had failed. With the exception of the social studies teacher (What a sexy angel she was!), all the teachers were angry at us while we students were angry at them for having given us such poor scores.

Our eccentric English teacher cussed us out. While he arranged his desk before continuing class, we quietly asked each other about our scores and sought solace. Our collective whispering turned the classroom into a fish market. "*Shut uuuuuup, damn it!*" We could have heard a pin drop after that. Mad as hell, he began writing the correct answers on the board for us to copy down. When his class was over, we turned to each other in disbelief about having fooled ourselves.

Here in the US, I can name so many who failed their driver's permit test because they believed that all it took was common sense. They had a thousand excuses for having failed. It's easy to ignore or violate the rules of the road, flee the scene of an accident, run from the cops, and resist arrest.

And so is taking a break after high school before going to college. But that can come back to bite us in the ass. Beware! Easy can be deceiving and bring drastic consequences.

Hard Is Easy and Rewarding

Usually, we pour all our energy into achieving goals that seem impossible to achieve but without which we would feel empty. Sure, some dreams do require a high level of commitment; the journey to win Olympic gold is an example. But in general, we sweat too much over life's hard issues. We spend countless hours preparing for a job interview we desperately need to nail. We toss and turn the night before, but we dress to kill and off we go. We're asked a couple of simple questions and get the job.

When we prepare for the worst, the best comes easily, so prepare; don't worry!

Overconfidence Can Be a Killer

When I was working on my private pilot's license, I flew through some real and metaphorical scary and bumpy weather. So many unexpected ups and downs and turns got so bad that I was close to giving up, but I'd spent way too much money and time on classes, and aviation was all I could see for a career. I had to go on. I forced myself to adjust to the reality I was facing—working the night shift and going to school in the morning—and I gained the confidence I needed. I progressed and improved. The jar of my confidence had no room for any more cookies.

The long-awaited time for a practical test came and found me on top of my game. The examiner and I went up for the flight exam. I nailed all the maneuvers, and she enjoyed a good flight, so I felt proud of myself. The sacrifices I had made were paying off, but I needed to focus on the task at hand—the flight exam—but I felt I was having the greatest day of my life. And then came time for her to get me lost and simulate an engine failure. She asked me to put the hood on, which I did.

"I'm going to slow the plane down, Arlindo."

"Okay," I said, as relaxed as a cat napping.

"I'm taking over," she said.

"Okay," I said again confidently. I knew what was coming next. She became the pilot in command for about ninety seconds and turned the plane sixty degrees off course. The game began.

"You can remove the hood now."

"All right," I said.

"Consider that we have an engine failure," she said.

"All right," I replied still on top of my game. I had practiced engine failures a ton of times usually with the engine running at idle, not just at a reduced speed as right then. I understood that she was being cautions regardless of the confidence I had shown because up there, things can go wrong fast, and dying is easier and quicker.

I followed the SOPs, which was to find the best gliding speed, sixty knots for the Cessna 152 we were flying. Piece of cake. Then I started looking for a place to land. To my surprise, there was an airport right in front of me. *Seriously? No need to sweat looking for a safe place to land? No way!* I thought.

I prepared to land at the airport, but two minutes later, she asked me to return to the airport we had taken off from. I was confused. She said, "You had an airport right there but you picked the wrong wind."

I'd flown into a headwind with engine failure instead of turning around and taking advantage of a tailwind that would have pushed me toward the airport we had left. The headwind would have made it impossible for me to make it to that second airport. I had been on a suicide mission.

We were both uncomfortable in the cockpit. I landed safely, exited the runway, and continued on the taxiway, sure I had failed the practical exam. I decided to break the silence by saying, "I'm sorry."

She cut me off. "Me too!"

She was mad as hell at me, but I was mad at her too for having given me a task way too easy to do. That's what had failed me. What stupidity! Who would take hard over easy?

I drove home cussing myself out and thinking about why I had done what I'd done, why I had failed such an easy task not realizing that my overconfidence was to blame. By that time, my overconfidence as well as my confidence had vanished. Worries about retaking the test started to sink in. I knew I'd lose many nights of sleep worrying about it.

On the day of the retest, I drove to the airport concerned and nervous. My examiner didn't seem mad at all, but I wasn't sure if she was just trying to keep things cool so I wouldn't be overwhelmed and do something stupider that could kill us or if she was truly not mad at me.

We took off, and right away, she asked me if I'd mind if she took over. I said, "No, I don't," but not understanding why she wanted to do that.

"I haven't flown this baby in a long time," she said.

I enthusiastically replied, "Oh, really? Go ahead. Take over!"

She was having fun. It's wasn't a lesson. It wasn't a test. It was pure enjoyment. She performed maneuvers that would have looked dangerous to nonpilots, but I was enjoying it as much as she was. We talked about my future as a pilot and blah blah blah. I was wondering when she was going to hand over the controls to me and start the retest. Well, that didn't happen. She headed back to the airport and landed. As she was taxiing, she handed me a paper. "Congratulations! And good luck," she said smiling as she watched out as she was supposed to for deer, birds, or planes trying to make emergency landings. No flight is over until everyone's out of the aircraft.

A million-pound brick was lifted off my chest. I was light as a feather and smiling broadly. My eyes caught hers. She was at that point the most beautiful, loving, and caring woman I'd ever seen. I wasn't sure if I wanted to hug her, kiss her, or cry to her. I wanted to be in her soul and let her share my happiness. "Thank you!" I said, and my eyes teared up. I'd reached a great milestone after some incredible sacrifices. I told myself, *Wow! She had passed me even before we got on the plane!* I knew I had failed the first time because of my overconfidence, not because she had made the test easy for me. I felt stupid until I glanced at the exam paper in my hands and smiled.

Never doubt your place in the game. Just to be part of the team is to be a winner. Take your mission seriously, and improve yourself even when you're at the top of your game or are ahead of the game. Carry a positive attitude with you to accomplish outstanding goals. Grab inspiration from other players. Always remember that what seems easy can be tricky and that overconfidence can be as bad as no confidence unless you understand and use your potential correctly. Give your best to the team and you'll never find yourself dancing with winners who didn't make the cut.

29

Winners Who Didn't Make the Cut

THERE ARE THREE RULERS BY which we can measure our successes and failures. The first is an objective ruler—society's expectations. If we meet expectations, we're great. If we deliver beyond expectations, we're heroes. This ruler can be pretty rude and unfair as it measures individual achievements against human powers of success without taking weak links into consideration. Yes, the world wants us to be great citizens with great minds, our friends want us to be best friends forever, and our families want us to be stars that shine on the family, but they could ignore our weakness and measure us inaccurately.

It doesn't matter how smart our siblings are; we can't be the greatest mathematicians, physicians, physicists, engineers, or astronomers if we inherited a learning disability or suffered a brain injury. We can't be great athletes if that's not in us. My father's smart. Although he didn't finish third grade, to this day, at age eighty-four, he still blames lack of money for his poor education. He brags about his learning ability and eagerness to learn. And I can see him as a very thoughtful clergy member. My mom didn't go to school. During her time, girls were to become great wives who raised beautiful families. Still, she has brains. And she's funny too. My brothers and sisters are all right.

We could feel like losers if we've been unable to make our dreams come true, and then society's expectations can add salt to our wounds. So unfortunate that we can't change the world. Fortunately, we can change ourselves.

The second measuring instrument for our success or failure is subjective—our dreams. The fewer dreams we turn into reality, the more we can count on being among those who didn't make the cut.

The third ruler is comparison. We find ourselves mad and frustrated when we see others with more than we have. Let's not do that; it's very detrimental to our advancement and joy. Measuring ourselves against others should empower us to work harder, not to punish ourselves. Greed can make us unsatisfied with what we have, and letting envy help determine if we're successful or not isn't wise or empowering.

Now, you can toss out all measurement methods to determine if you're a big winner or a winner who didn't make the cut and make an honest assessment of your journey taking into consideration all the factors in your control as well as those out of your control. If you like where you stand, carry on. Otherwise, make adjustments. If you're twenty-nine and without a place to stay, jobless, and illiterate, be humble and honest. You're a winner who didn't make the cut… yet. Distinguished professors and lawyers and gifted athletes who ended up homeless didn't make the cut or made it but lost it probably right when they desperately needed to be winners. People who spent most of their lives as criminals obviously didn't make the cut. If you live where the sun never shines, you're a winner who didn't make the cut. If you're retired, relying on just a pension, and living with your daughter, you didn't make the cut either.

Avoid such drama. Don't wait until you're on your deathbed to assess your journey; do so while you have time to make adjustments, and don't let that frighten you. Make a greater effort to accomplish your dreams. Do your best to minimize your frustration, and hope for the dark clouds to lift. Be aware that we all tend to underestimate our successes and undermine the reasons for our failures. Be realistic and accept the outcome of your actions. Your goal should be to enjoy your life to the last breath. There's no "Oh thanks! I didn't make the cut. I guess I'm a fucking loser, right? I don't give a shit. I'm gonna die a loser, and that's fine with me." That attitude should be killed at birth.

We've have been conditioned to compete on high levels set by people with strength, wealth, and possibilities. To be a winner is no longer a game of just dedication; it's a nightmare unless we read between the lines and fill in the blanks.

Walk your walk while appreciating what you've achieved and stay focused on achieving more without stress and frustration. And definitely do not look at what the guys next to you are having for dinner unless that will inspire you to do better so you can afford what they're eating.

As we age, life gets more complicated and our means of surviving and achieving success diminish, but we can always watch out for threats and grab opportunities. Life's a bitch that becomes bitchier when we're driven by unrealistic expectations. Just be sure you don't let your powers stay dormant, walk away from any challenge, or give up on any quest. Go with your thirst for more and better within your possibilities. Stay true to yourself, your powers, threats and opportunities, and stay focused on collecting all the apples, oranges, and lemons you can to make yourself delicious juices.

If you're a winner who didn't make the cut and it's too late to remedy the situation, don't let that sour, depressing sentiment take away your joy of life. A time will come when nothing matters other than the enjoyment of your last meals whether you're the winner of all winners or a winner who didn't make the cut. Your joy of life will follow you to the grave. Your great achievements will stay behind for others to enjoy. And your failures are for others to cuss out. With that said, fear not—The game isn't over yet.

30

Game Over

WHEN WE'RE WINNING OR THE game is fun, we don't want to go home. Even when the game is not that exciting, we don't want it to end. We keep hoping that it'll change and give us time to score big. But sadly, life can deal cards that sometimes make us wish the game was over. We've played our best but still lose and want out of it.

Well, we should play as best we can until the game is over.

At age ninety, you aren't much of a player and shouldn't be trying to play as if you were still an MVP; the game is faster and harder while you're slower and weaker. You're holding low cards, but you can still play them even if you can't win big with them.

If you never liked the game, now is the time to play it. You've reached the finish line. You're by all means part of the mystery. You're playing alongside legendary creatures. Whatever the human journey is, you're part of it. Now that you see the finish line, think, *Angels fly because they take themselves lightly.* You shouldn't be sitting at the table cussing at the game and the players; instead, say, "We're all winners at birth" and finish your ride with pride and happiness. Don't make the last stretch of your journey a frustrating experience of regrets and disappointments. Focus on enjoying every bit of your remaining time for the game.

Your mind should be clear.

Your heart should be loving.

Your spirit should be at peace.

You have after all danced with life on different dance floors even when the songs weren't great. Now is time to enjoy slow dancing until the DJ calls "Last song!" Only then will you know that the game is over. Remind yourself that when you leave, you'll be missed. Of that you can be sure!

A Moment of Reflection

That thing we call happiness. Each day, happiness changes its face, shape, and ways making it very hard for us to find solid ground for defining it. If that's not daunting enough, our finances—one of the main ingredients of happiness—has been strictly controlled by capitalism, the best economic system for individual prosperity, growth, and happiness.

What's wrong with this picture, though, is unless we understand the games going on behind the scenes, capitalism will drive us to spend all our treasure and time on building castles that by the time they're done, we're unable to live in them. So dream big dreams that require low maintenance. Make as many small dreams come true as you can; they're the path to big achievements. Don't drop dead trying to live; be living while you're trying to live. Prioritize your health, nutrition and fitness since they're the pedestal of happiness. You know it well—a lonely man with a pocket full still lives an empty life, and a rich man in poor health is destitute of life. Then, you might want to try a small life filled with bits of happiness instead of a large, empty life filled with stress, frustration, and dissatisfaction.

Keep your heart warm whatever it takes. Make sure that your sexual desires or at least your basic sexual needs are covered. As is the case with many other aspects of life, only you know what your basic sexual needs are. Don't measure yourself against others especially when you can't see the sources of their success. Anytime you let others and their achievements spell happiness for you, you contribute to their happiness at the expense of yours. Care for the birds in your hand instead of the two flying by. Respect that, and live a happy life defined by your words, wisdom, and grit.

&&&

Ahead of the game and far behind time. This is a situation when you have things under control; life has to catch up to you while you're too young for time that's yours. Say you're forty-five and have already saved enough to retire but you're still playing as if you were twenty-one; you're ahead of the game. Or you're fifty-two with health as good as someone half your age; you're ahead of the game; you're living far younger than so many others are. You've made sacrifices to get to where you are, and you feel empowered, happy, and successful. Good nutrition, health, fitness, and well-managed finances have put you ahead of the game and far behind time.

&&&

Behind the game and far behind time. Here you are at twenty-seven fooling around with rapping and sure you'll make it big because your friends tell you that you will. Shows you do at little venues for promotion instead of money are poisoned lollypops you're happy to suck on. So far, you've been fooled by some pretty girls who had been brought with free entry and free drinks and possibly some cash in their bras to go crazy at your shows so you'll come back again and again for less. The tragedy is that before you know it, your fortieth birthday will arrive and find you behind the game and far behind your time, still trying to make it, but still frustrated and disappointed when you look around and see what your buddies have accomplished—good jobs, happy families. Things will not be easy for you.

This little example is not for wannabe rappers only; it's for all of us dancing with promising fantasies without taking matters seriously, measuring our progress, or being aware of our stagnation. Imagine being a twenty-two-year-old guy without a driver's license, not working, not going to college, a virgin who stays home playing video games and chatting with online friends including a nineteen-year-old girl without a driver's license who works part time at a fast-food place, a virgin who spends all her time on social media; those two are behind the game and far behind time. Millennials who haven't taken advantage of all that technology and life have to offer them and have no dreams are behind the game and far behind time too. These people will become thirty-six, then sixty, then eighty-two in the same state—not empowered, not in relationships, frustrated, and still behind the game and far behind time.

Get your game going as soon as you can. If you're young, get and stay ahead of the game. It's not a sin to be behind the game and behind time, but it can be unforgiving.

&&&

Human stupidity... What's up with that? I can't wait for world to be governed by robots and artificial intelligence. We have so far done a terrible job of that. Instead of gathering and coming up with great ways to ensure fairness and happy and peaceful lives for all, some pour all their resources into becoming leaders of a dominant world power. As a result, people live oppressed and in poverty, and nations go to war. Sadly, robots and artificial intelligence will not take over before we immigrate to space. On the other hand, maybe men will have a change of heart sooner and treat their fellow human beings with respect and dignity. My doubts are strong, though, because men love stupidity.

We take so many actions before determining the consequences, and we do that often. We pull out $100 from an ATM just to impress our friends and pay a $35 fee for an overdraft. We entertain friends who come over when we receive welfare checks to smoke weed and borrow some cash from us, and we don't get it back. We know how bad drugs, drinking, and smoking anything are bad for us, addictive, and expensive, but we keep on with those vices. We eat poorly, keep on doing that, and become diabetics with bad hearts. Why's this if we're the ultimate species with great intellectual powers?

We waste water by taking long showers. We trash our leftovers. We spend way too much on our rides with custom rims. We buy expensive homes that we can't afford, and we worry about losing them. We live way beyond our means and stress out about catching up. We're afraid of becoming poor, and we envy the rich; that can lead us to living lives of crime, grabbing for power, and exploiting others. We know we're being stupid, but we still act stupidly especially in the heat of some moments. We try to keep our stupidity under control and avoid causing trouble for ourselves, but we still get ourselves into trouble. We should train ourselves to walk away from senseless arguments and keep our cool.

When stupidity gets you in trouble, life's laughing at you. You can't punch life in the mouth. Just consider bad situations as lessons learned, get back on track, and be aware that stupidity is lurking for opportunities to strike again; don't make that easy for it to do.

&&&

Little things of big value. We are wired to appreciate little things. We like spending time with our children, and they like spending time with us. Our parents taught us to show others our love, respect, and appreciation for them, and we and our friends want the same. We should not miss opportunities to show love, respect, and appreciation to our children, parents, and friends; those are gifts from the heart that we can give one another.

When you give from your heart instead of from the world, your gifts are better appreciated, and you won't go broke giving them. Giants may be strong and powerful, but only ants can carry 150 times their body weight.

&&&

Where's enough? Enough is nowhere to be found because enough is never enough, and it's always hiding. We have evolved to be constantly looking for the next better thing, which can be rewarding, exciting, and empowering and can improve our lives. But if we're never satisfied, we'll end up dissatisfied. It makes no sense to strive for more if the process takes away our ability to enjoy what we have.

Let's always be growing as we indulge in what we have, and let's never forget that when we improve what we have to elite status, we'll have more than enough and become more empowered to get more. Greed under control is a good thing; it expands our wings and extends our scope. We can use that to propel ourselves to new wonders.

&&&

Mysteries of the mystery. Life is an unwinding of mysteries that began with mysteries. Science can't prove many things, and we can make only guesses based on our ignorance. Good and bad luck, curses, Friday the thirteenth, black cats crossing our paths, opening umbrellas in the house, when it rains, it pours, astrology, witchcraft, ghosts, and so on are superstitions. People said that the *Titanic* sunk because man had jinxed it by boasting, "Not even God himself could sink it."

Vibes—both good and bad—get passed on. Those surrounded by good people will pick up their good vibes and pass them along, and the reverse is true as well; bad vibes can take people down. At times, we're on edge and stressed out but don't know why. It has nothing to do with a full moon, PMS, or the bad dinner we had the night before. We sense bad vibes, but we simply can't figure where they're coming from. We should make sure that whatever we do empowers us whether it's based on superstitions or not.

Don't hate those whose philosophies differ from yours; life and let live.

&&&

Failure and success are both great. Failure is a success because when we fail, that shows we tried. But sadly, fear of failure is ingrained in us; we don't want to fail because that makes us feel stupid and incompetent. We never reflect on the truth of the matter: failure is great because it leads to success. Therefore, when we fail, we should get ourselves back on track and focused on success because success will not just land in our laps.

Mistakes and perfection share meals from the very plate of failure and success. We will all fail repeatedly, but we can all keep aiming at perfection however we define it. It's our duty to investigate why we fail not to beat ourselves up but to improve ourselves so that we can succeed and celebrate that.

&&&

The platform. Having a purpose in life is a must; it's something we should always keep in mind and review daily particularly when we face nasty surprises, unpredictability, distress, etc. Our purposes should be philosophical principles that lead to success, happiness, peace, and brotherhood; our purposes should be our mentors, wells from which we draw strength and wisdom.

Whether your platform is prayer, a notebook filled with insightful words, inspirational sentences, and powerful quotations, or simply serenity of your spirit, stay on your platform as much as you can, and avoid worldly temptations that could pull you off it. Your platform keeps you focusing on the path to success and avoiding the clowns on the curb.

When you don't have a firm platform, you'll find yourself copying others' platforms and thus living by their standards and values rather than yours.

&&&

Life sucks. Our parents had fun during sex, and without our permission, our fathers threw us into the battle of the sperm. We are the result of the one sperm who won the race that caused our first birth—insemination—but we had to stay where we were for nine months before we were born again and were able to cry, scream, kick, and wail—good signs of our normality What a wonderful way to welcome life! Some religions take this as testimony for their preaching that life must endure pain and suffering to get salvation and eternal peace and glory after death.

For our first four or so years, we worked hard to become toddlers, and we told our parents that we didn't want to grow up. And then before we knew it, the world was slapping us hard as hell because we'd changed from adorable angels to little devils. And in a blink of an eye, we entered the boxing ring of life starting with school.

Let's forget being forced to learn so much nonsense that didn't empower us; let's reflect on our mean teachers, bullies, racism, discrimination, school lunches, and all the other things that made us want to puke that teamed up to make us wish school evaporated alongside all teachers and students. Education sharpened its horns every day while we were getting pissed off for having to face them. The nightmare was that victory there was directly proportional to the economic power of our parents and/or potential of our country, which by the way dictates or gives us clues as to how our fight in other rings of life could be.

Systematic racism, discrimination, and other forms of social unfairness are still the main reason students say that school sucks. With poverty dominating most social classes worldwide ever since we can remember, just about every poor student hated school.

And we had no idea about the big monster waiting for us: puberty, the most unmerciful phase of life especially for girls. The physical and physiological changes we went through were brutal. Around every corner was a whip ready to sting us. Dodging them, battling the push and pull with our parents and siblings, and dealing with society's brutality, ignorance, and stupidity made life no Disney World. How could we not hate everybody and be mad about everything?

And as soon as we found freedom (at age eighteen for some and at age twenty-one for others), we found out that we were not that free; we had social laws, rules, and regulations to obey and follow.

The next bout in the ring was finding and holding a job; that meant more rules and regulations imposed on us by our bosses and having to put up with coworkers at unfulfilling jobs that didn't pay us what we were worth, and that was frustrating.

And with our relationships, instead of enjoying them, we went through countless hellish days and nightmares before we reached the boiling point and settled matters in the court. It seemed that child support and alimony would doom us.

On the other side of the relationship river, after bouncing from one relationship to another with hearts full of scars, we lived the single life without sex or embraced relationships only for sex and some companionship as long as that would last. In that boxing ring, we pulled our boots on to raise families, but then many of us saw our children drift away from the path to higher education due to the lack of financial resources or due to being hypnotized by the media and tech companies with their poisoned lollypops. If we rode blindfolded on slippery roads and had bad falls, we could've found ourselves battling the nightmares of drug addiction, and worse yet, seeing our sons and daughters leave this world way too soon due to drug overdoses. There isn't a greater pain than that caused by having to bury your children. Life sucks.

If we made it to middle age, our health would have been ruined by the food and drink big corporations supplied us with and charged us for. That combined with bad genes and lack of exercise could make our lives a living hell. Even if we had inherited the best genes and exercised and ate right, we were at the mercy of polluted environments and the natural aging process. When we're unhealthy and taking care of our sick parents, we're really dead. Life really sucks. We're battling hypertension, high cholesterol, cardiovascular disease, and so on, which seem as unavoidable as is aging. This burden gets heavier each day, and its consequences are directly proportional to our financial states. For people living where the sun never shines, there aren't enough words and F-bombs to describe how much life sucks.

At age thirteen, we dreamed of becoming rich, marrying the most beautiful girl in town or the most handsome man in the world, living in a mansion, traveling the world, and in general living large. At age twenty-five, we're still dreaming those dreams, but when we hit seventy, we ask ourselves, *Where the fuck did all the time go? What about all my dreams?*

In our final years, we enter the last ring not having really lived as we had imagined we should have. By then, we're just hoping it will be all over soon and wondering, *Where was the thrill of life?* The journey of life was nothing more than being born, facing human stupidity, suffering, and dying.

According to this analysis, there's no thrill on the journey of life, but this analysis is biased and full of prejudice. The journey of life started with the first single cell about 4.5 billion years ago. From there, the tree of life grew, evolved, and mutated all the way to us—modern legends. The thrills of life are diverse and infinite. We see life as a journey that sucks simply because we stay behind the game and fail to read between the lines and fill in the blanks. We also fail ourselves by neglecting our duties and not taking the game seriously.

Regardless of how blessed or cursed we are, life sucks if we let it run its course, and it's great if we take our destiny in our own hands. Life sucks only if we have no purpose. If we find and pursue our purpose, life will never suck. Every time life shows us a suck-face, we should clear the fog from our eyes and see life clearly for what it is—something extraordinarily mysterious and joyful. That isn't easy; it requires our critical thinking—reading between the lines and filling in the blanks.

Nature provides for us with few strings attached while what man provides for us comes with many strings attached. Nature speaks beauty, health, and purity while man speaks money and sarcasm. Use your wisdom and grit to make nature your best friend, and watch out for man.

The almighty God is gracious to nature and man alike and ensures that each receives the share they deserve for they both plant seeds of health, wealth, and happiness along the road of the human journey.

The bottom line is that life's good, beautiful, and breathtaking as well as bad, ugly, and horrifying. It's your responsibility to stay safe and live happily. Free your mind, obey your desires, be creative, and indulge in the joys of life and you'll have no time to think or say, "Life sucks."

Tips

People understand that shit happens, but no one understands it on the highway. Everybody wants to get to their destination on time, so don't give in to road rage literally or figuratively.

Use your common sense, wisdom, and grit to stay alive and living. Whether you're the cause or the consequence of your troubles and difficulties, don't respond in kind.

Don't linger at your friend's house after the game is over especially if your spouse is waiting for you.

Don't ask too many questions about your friends' boyfriends or girlfriends or say you know them very well; that will just trigger questions.

Don't cuss out the destitute for not strapping their boots on once all they have is shoelaces. Instead, give them sandals to ease their circumstances.

Respect the numbers. Manage your finances carefully in good times and in bad. Make the sacrifices you need to make for your finances and for other areas of life. Just getting by isn't cutting it anymore because there are too many powerful agents trying to throw you off course.

Every story has two sides, so don't let the darkness of something blind you to its light. Steer your ship away from troubled waters, quarantine your demons, and have sympathy for the victims of demons.

Find inspiration and empowerment in your idols and other charismatic individuals, but keep in mind that they can have dark sides.

Be the best at whatever you do. So many end up doing lame work after they've spent a ton of money and time earning higher educations. Do whatever you are doing to the best of your ability, and empower yourself for greatness ahead.

The bird in your hand can fly away if you take a nap; don't take it for granted. Protect and grow what you have being aware that time can change everything.

Whispering forgiveness into the ears of loved ones in a coma is showing empathy a bit too late. Don't let feuds with family or friends fester. Find common ground, settle your differences, and restore love as soon as possible.

Slow down to go fast.

Things Worth Noting

Great nations and people aren't great for doing great things; they're great for doing great things right.

White lies are harmless until they are spoken.

Be with the best so you can be the best.

Worship all who bring happiness to your heart and peace to your soul.

School sucks until you face the ignorance of illiterates.

Stay a fair distance from your enemies while you keep them in place of your friends.

Life's a bitch, and you're a big dog.

To accept sour events as part of empowerment is to move toward excellence.

You're very small and powerless until you see your true self—big and invincible.

The sighted are kings in the land of the blind, but the blind are masters of darkness.

A great loser is a winner for he tried his best.

See no evil through the devil's eyes.

Be aggressively greedy on your pursuit and then gracious in your victory.

Live as if today is your greatest day, not your last.

Like it or not, you live only once, so make it count!

Afterword

You might not care that God created us the way he did as well as what surrounds us, or that after billions of years of evolution, we're eyewitnesses to the greatness of all greatness—life. Never let go of the invisible emblem on your chest: "This special emblem is the symbol of my heroism because I am a winner. I am a winner because I was born. I am a special because I am a hero."

For reasons I believe we'll never find out, we're the elite of evolution, the masterpiece of all masterpieces, and the only masterpiece endowed with brains to see, analyze, create, and seize opportunities. We're the only species capable of preventing its extinction and the extinction of all other species. We're the only ones holding the keys to all the treasure boxes of life. Every day is a reason for celebration. We're God's most beloved sons and daughters to whom the greatest blessing were given to keep life going. We've been trying hard to understand our mystery and the mystery of it all. We've come a long way, and the road ahead is endless. We're the special travelers on that endless road. We're the ones!

Since a hundred years is too short a time for us to unleash our power to its maximum, we ought to cash in on everything we can. If we answer the call of duty, we'll improve the quality of our lives and achieve more and sooner.

We might not all be cut out for building spaceships, but we're all cut out for something great. We can look into our soul and find our treasure boxes. We can achieve whatever we put our minds to and inspire others.

If you've tried your best and still find yourself going nowhere fast, reconsider your approach to life. Find the problems, fix them, and replace your threats with opportunities. You have a large amount of knowledge and power; it's time to put them to work. Develop your skills in reading between the lines and filling in the blanks. If there's something you want, go get it. If there's a will, there's a way. If you can think it, you can do it.

Don't fool yourself, and don't let anyone else fool you that you can snap a finger and your dreams will become reality. When determination, commitment, and perseverance are the voices and companions you've chosen to walk with and you stay focused and true to your goals, you will get to your destination safe and sound and happily collect the rewards awaiting you.

Be smart and enjoy your trophies. Embark on your next journey meant to increase your growth and expand your abilities, and enjoy life with greater satisfaction. As the North Star you are, you can't hide behind clouds or allow any obstructions in your path. You must shine because your glory and survival of all people depend on the light you shed. There's no chaos to deter you, nor do you have time for negative voices.

Your game is demanding, but your attitude is strong. You have places to go and faces to see. You have a mission to accomplish. When you run out of inspiration and energy, reach into the miracle box for support and then continue your journey. The moment you realized that you've been a winner since birth, a hero with specialties, you embraced your gifts and promised to play harder and continuously. You survived rough waters and many obstacles. You tangoed with life. You put on great shows when the music was upbeat and the stage was smooth as well as when the music sucked, the dance floor was cracked, and you were wearing worn-out shoes. And your partner wasn't even a great dancer. Nothing could stop you. You knew that your twisted ankle would heal and that in no time, you'd be putting on great shows again. You did, and you're still growing and dancing.

Each of us has dormant potential that if awakened would better our lives and the lives of our brothers and sisters. Don't fear the beast. Grab life by the horns and just dance with it in celebration. You live only once, so make it count.

If you feel that life's laughing at you and hasn't given you what you want, get it yourself and then shout at life that you see no clowns in the room but life itself. And if people are refusing to grant you access to the doors of opportunity, force yourself in wisely or discover a back door, get what you want, and then utter, "I wanna see you try to stop me now!"

Each day, this game brings something new, ugly, and unpleasant as well as new ways of making our journey easier. It also gives us better tools to help us get to our destinations quicker, safer, and happier. We've come far, and we'll go farther. When we can no longer carry the torch of humanity, our descendants will.

As part of the process of keeping human excellence marching to infinity, you, as a great participant in this march, could feel disempowered, wounded, and desperate, but it's not acceptable to let those feelings paralyze you. Fight them off. Never allow the shadows of death to block your confidence, determination, or grit. The wiser you are, the easier your journey should be for you've been there and done that. What's yet to be seen will not escape your sight; your wisdom has given you binoculars to read between the lines and fill in the blanks to stay ahead of the game.

If you find yourself unsatisfied with life or behind the game, be realistic about your threats and opportunities and look at the cards in your hands. Evaluate their worth and go on with the game. Play hard, and play smart. Remind yourself constantly that you can turn any losing hand into a gracious victory. You are after all a power that evolved from great to greater and then to the greatest. You are part of the journey of no match.

We, the modern humans, are the man. Let's drink to that and celebrate until the day we say goodbye and cross over. There's a little space for each of us to play. Find yours, and wiggle to the end.

Author's Note

I AS WELL AS MANY others have gone through the thrills as well as the abysses of life. If you haven't gone through an abyss, I'm not sure you're enjoying life to the fullest. Yet as long as your purpose and duties are fulfilled and you're cherishing happiness, you'll be all right.

We all can use our abilities to achieve success and excellence; we just need to pay attention to what's an important part of our makeup but something we've been ignoring or giving too little attention to—reading between the lines and filling in the blanks. Those are powers we used to survive ever since we were in the jungles of Africa.

When animals we hadn't seen before approached us, we looked for clues to help us decide to flee them, fight them, or ignore them. That was reading between the lines and filling in the blanks. Later, that ability helped us decide whether someone we were attracted to would make us happy. Reading between the lines and filling in the blanks are part of our makeup; those powers help us stay ahead of the game and cherish life.

In this last volume of *Stay Ahead of the Game* trilogy, I did my best to show the importance of reading between the lines and filling in the blanks, and I hope I haven't fallen short. I also hope you get your hands on books such as this one that will help you understand the journey of life, and I hope you use everything in your power to enjoy life and be successful.

Whether or not you're glad to be born, you're part of humanity. Do your best to enjoy the journey as much as you can starting today no matter your age. We're cherishing the best of humanity. Don't let your share go to waste.

Acknowledgments

I THANK GOD, MY MOM, Feliciana Gomes Tavares, and my dad, Manuel Moreno Fernandes, for life, wisdom, and grit. I thank my brothers, Jorge and Joao, and my sisters Cecilia, Dasneves, and Fatima and the rest of my family especially my aunt Eduarda (Talvina) for the love, care, and appreciation they have shown me.

I thank my sons Claudio, William, Carlos, and Christopher for their love, care, abuse, and disrespect, which made us best friends forever. I also thank Catarina and Angela, mothers of my sons, for being there. I thank Jaquelina and Severa (Mavera) for pushing me to go on strong. I thank Saesar, Aniya, and Ava for the innocent, unconditional baby love they have shown me. (Saesar, you are my heart, and I love you too).

I thank my brothers-in-law Jose Maria (Ze), Jose Manuel Carvalho Silva (Ze) and Mario and sister-in-law Matilde. My grandparents Rosa Vieira and Paulo Gomes, my aunt and godmother Benvinda, and Vera, my mother-in-law, you're dearly missed. Rest in peace. I thank philosopher Sergio Pinto, Jose Luis (Ze Luis) for all the good times and the writing inspiration. I thank special friends Pedro Barros, Adalberto Costa, Aida Duarte, Angela, Tuja, Marinha, Helena and Alberto. I really appreciated the friendship, wisdom and inspiration. Luisa Lobo, I can never thank you enough for showing me the way to making my greatest dream (becoming a pilot) come true. I thank pilot Avelino Barros for the thrills of flying and Eugenio Rodrigues for the thrills and inspiration in music. I thank my two best female friends Chomsaeng Khattiya and May Astin for the unconditional friendship and inspiration.

I thank all my readers for their unconditional support. I am glad to have finished the *Stay Ahead of the Game* trilogy, which was possible thanks to the support shown in many ways, shapes, and forms I received from each of you individually and collectively, directly and indirectly.

Last but not least, I thank iUniverse, my publishing company, for a job well done.

My special appeal goes to all youngsters. It doesn't matter who or where you are, you can distinguish yourself once you embrace the reality and possibilities of life and become excellent. The world may not have equal opportunities for all, but it has opportunities for all. Just because you might live in a poor country and have no means to immigrate to a country with diversified opportunities doesn't mean your wings are broken without the possibility of healing, nor does living in a rich country mean you can just sit and watch your dreams come true.

Start your journey as soon as possible, and stay committed to your objectives. The turtle won the race because steady she went, and the rabbit lost because she went fast but fooled around on the way.

Whatever your dreams are, there are three supporting beams you must have: a good education, solid finances, and satisfying relationships, so understand their importance; that will give you a strong start on your journey. People in power are committed to taking over your destiny, so don't allow that to happen. Be in charge of your destiny throughout; it takes sacrifice to be a winner. The current times offer many opportunities and prizes, but your competitors will be numerous. Be aggressively greedy during your pursuit but then be humble in your victory. You youngsters carry the torch of human greatness. We're counting on you because you're more gifted and powerful than we are and all generations before us were.

And on that note, I thank my niece Neiva Naidine Fernandes De Brito (Telma) for her great, continuous support. She's my greatest inspiration, my hero.

Until we meet again, accept my best wishes for you all. Life's a game. Let's win it!

Printed in the United States
by Baker & Taylor Publisher Services